SMART Money Grant Writing:

Get the Funding Your Organization Needs and Deserves

By Tarra Nystrom, MBA, CBA

My Cup of T Press

Text copyright © 2020

Tarra Nystrom

All rights reserved.

No part of this book may be reproduced, stored in a retrieval system, or transmitted in any form or by any means (electronic, mechanical, photocopying, recording, or otherwise), without expressed written permission of this publisher and author.

This publication is designed to provide accurate and authoritative information in regard to the subject matter covered. It is sold with the understanding that the publisher and author are not engaged in rendering legal or accounting services. If legal advice or other expert assistance is required, the services of a competent professional person should be sought.

Published by My Cup of T Press Columbus, Ohio

ISBN: 13-978-1-7360720-1-1

Library of Congress number: On file

Printed in the United States of America

Dedicated to Steven and Jessica

SMART Money Grant Writing:

Get the Funding Your Organization Needs and Deserves

Blocks of Content

How to Use This Book i

What to Know Before Writing a Grant Proposal

What Is a Grant? 2

The Basics and Beyond 13

Getting Grant Ready 35

Finding and Vetting Grant Opportunities 49

Let's Write the Grant Proposal

Cover Letters and Cover Sheets for Grant Proposals 61

Organizational Information for Grant Proposals 67

Mission Statements for Grant Proposals 69

Needs Statements for Grant Proposals 71

Program/Project Descriptions for Grant Proposals 79

Program/Project Evaluations for Grant Proposals 86

Budgets for Grant Proposals 91

Financials for Grant Proposals 104

Executive Summaries for Grant Proposals 108

Partnerships, In-Kind Donations, and Volunteer

      Information for Grant Proposals 112

Attachments for Grant Proposals 120

Logic Models for Grant Proposals 124

Data and Metrics for Grant Proposals 142

Storytelling for Grant Proposals 163

Polish the Proposal 175

Research Resources for Grant Proposals 180

Managing the Grant Proposal Writing Process

Grants Management 187

Wellness for Grant Proposal Writing Professionals 196

Hiring and Being Hired as A Grant Proposal Writer 200

The Program 209

About the Author 217

How to Use This Book

I wrote *SMART Money Grant Writing*: *Get the Funding Your Organization Needs and Deserves* to help you become a better grant proposal writer. I wrote each topic as a block of information (instead of a chapter) to build a solid grant proposal writing foundation. Blocks are useful on their own to elevate oneself, or they combine to be a part of a foundation, exactly as each block in this book is intended. Each block can be read on its own to bolster skills or learn more about a particular part of the grant proposal writing process. And every block has valuable tips and tricks to establish a comprehensive skill set and build a solid foundation.

It is great to read how to refine a craft, such as grant proposal writing. It is even better when there are examples and samples from which to train and learn. The standard practice in training is to provide authentic illustrations and archetypes. The standard is also that a variety of examples are presented, but this standard creates little or no continuity for training or lessons covering multiple modules or chapters (or blocks); there is no frame of reference from which to build. Variety can be good, but continuity provides a better understanding and base. Therefore, every example is from the same program, Mentoring Individuals with Disabilities' Flip It Reverse Job and Career Fair. The details of this program at found at the end of the book.

Throughout *SMART Money Grant Writing* and from The Program, note that "want to be working" is consistently referenced for our target constituency. In this specific program, there is a discernable difference between people with disabilities, people with disabilities who are unemployed, and people with disabilities who are unemployed but want to be working.

Variety of word use is also expected throughout most nonfiction writing—not so in *SMART Money Grant Writing*. Clever and varied prose makes for more exciting reading. However, you are not here to be entertained. You bought this book to learn. Over 13 years of training grant proposal writers, I realize that using a bunch of different words for the sake of variety sometimes confuses explanations. This is what I mean: The word *inputs* will always refer to program or project resources. Intentionally, the words *program* and *project* rarely appear by themselves. Too many apprenticed grant proposal writers get hung up about which one they talk. While each is defined independently, any organization can call it whatever they want. Although the persistent and consistent use of the same program/project terminology throughout this book might seem mundane, it diminishes confusion.

Another deliberate use of words limits the use of the terms *goals*, *objectives*, and *outcomes*. This trio causes more confusion than any other in the nonprofit world. For your training purposes, the goal is the organization's mission, objectives are forgotten, and outcomes take on a more specific role than you once thought. Instead, the terms *inputs, activities, outputs, outcomes*, and *impacts* take their place.

As grant proposal writing skills are honed throughout these blocks, understand that *community* is conceptual as well as geographical.

Last but most importantly, *SMART Money Grant Writing* was written to help you work SMARTer, not harder, managing your organization's grant process. Most project management can be split into identifiable specific, measurable, achievable, relevant, and time-bound actions. Grant proposal writing IS project management, and it too should be SMART. Throughout the training, every component of grants management is clarified with specific, measurable, achievable, relevant, and time-bound propositions.

Whether you seek grant money for a nonprofit organization, a for-profit business venture, or individual funding for art or writing endeavors, submitting a well-written effort best positions you to be awarded the funding your organization needs and deserves. Let's start writing SMARTer.

What to Know Before Writing a Grant Proposal

What is a Grant?

What Is a Grant?
>A grant is a sales proposal.
>
>A grant is networking, an invitation to partner and build a relationship.
>
>A grant is a contract.
>
>A grant is a catalyst for building credibility and elevating the reputation in your community and with other funders.
>
>A grant is a competition.
>
>A grant is part of the lifeblood of your organization's funding strategy.
>
>A grant is a logical call to action.
>
>A grant is a demonstration of advocacy—for the grantee and grantor.
>
>A grant is for public relations and advertising.
>
>A grant is SMART.
>
>And you thought a grant was just free money!

To execute any endeavor for the most success, you must understand what the endeavor is all about. Let's look at why a grant is each of these things. We will go into much greater detail about each throughout the *SMART Money Grant Writing* blocks.

A grant is a sales proposal. A proposal is a plan put forward for consideration; a business or sales proposal is a written offer. A grant proposal is a plan that articulates and substantiates a case for need, points a way forward with a program or project, and postulates the expected outcomes and impacts. You are making a pitch. A sales proposal lets you pitch a product or service to land new or repeat business. In this case, the new or repeat business is a grant award (whether a new award or a renewed one). Like a sales proposal, the grant application is a written offer from the grant seeker for partnership with the grantmaker.

A grant is networking, an invitation to partner and build a relationship. Networking is a supportive system of sharing information among individuals and groups having a common interest. Business networking is a socioeconomic business activity by which business people meet to form business relationships, recognize, create, or act upon business opportunities, share information, and seek potential partners for ventures. By submitting a grant proposal, you are engaging a prospective funding partner in your business opportunity. The opportunity or venture is the program/project for which you need support. The program/project is the shared action in which the partnership is founded and upon which a relationship can be built. The relationship is fostered more quickly if the award is made. Even if the grant is not awarded, more people with a shared interest know about your program/project and organization.

A grant is a contract. A contract is an agreement between two or more parties for a specified activity and time, in most cases enforceable by law. It is a formal, written agreement. A grant proposal sets the guidelines (the inputs, expected outcomes, and anticipated impacts) of the program/project and is a formal, written agreement for partnership with the grantmaker. The agreement stipulates the organization will use the grantmaker's money to conduct certain activities, utilizing specified inputs (resources), achieving expected results of particular impacts tied to the mission intended to improve upon or eliminate a need in the community. Typically, the terms of this contract are realized through the conferring of funds to the organization and the organization's implementation, completion, and evaluation of the program/project.

A grant is a catalyst for building credibility and elevating your reputation in the community and with other funders. A catalyst is a person or thing that triggers an event. Credibility is the quality of being believable or trustworthy. Reputation is public or broad recognition of one's status. Because the need addressed by your program/project is evidence-based and thoroughly planned, your succinctly written grant proposal can now be the thing that makes it happen—the catalyst. The ability to convincingly and authentically demonstrate need and explain how the need will be improved upon or eliminated by program/project implementation will make you the expert in your community, showing that your organization can be trusted to most prudently use the funder's money. Productive partnerships also boost credibility and reputation. Grant awards are effective partnerships because they show other potential funders that another supports the value of the program/project and organization, likewise, within the community.

A grant is a competition. Unless the organization is the sole invitee for a solicited proposal, the grant proposal will compete for the funding made available by the grantor. Competition is to strive to outdo another for acknowledgment or a prize. Other organizations have well-planned programs/projects, excellent track records, and submit fantastic proposals just as you do. Your program/project probably is not wholly original, and another group in the area is likely to be providing similar or related services or products. Your submission must outdo the others in substance and style to be the most competitive.

A grant is part of the lifeblood of your organization's funding strategy. Since a strategy is a plan of action or policy designed to achieve a significant or overall purpose, common sense tells you that a funding strategy is your organization's plan to fund the budget fully. A funding strategy will include all and diverse revenue streams, including but not limited to: Grants, individual donations, planned and legacy giving, fundraising events, capital campaigns, in-kind gifts, volunteer value, interest, and fee-based programs, products, or services. A well-regarded industry standard for sustainability is that the grants' funding piece of the (funding) strategy pie should be no more than 30%. That is why I refer to it as part of the lifeblood of your organization's funding strategy. Every budget item for the organization, including its programs/projects, needs to be paid for with a combination of money and in-kind support. Funding is a supply of money. A grant is funding for a program/project or any other funding need for your nonprofit's operation. Let's look at a sample funding strategy on the next page.

Sample Funding Strategy
Fiscal Year 20**

Grants—20%
Fundraising—18%
Fee-based Services—16%
Private Donations—15%

In-kind Donations—15%
Volunteer Value—10%
Planned Giving—4%
Interest—2%

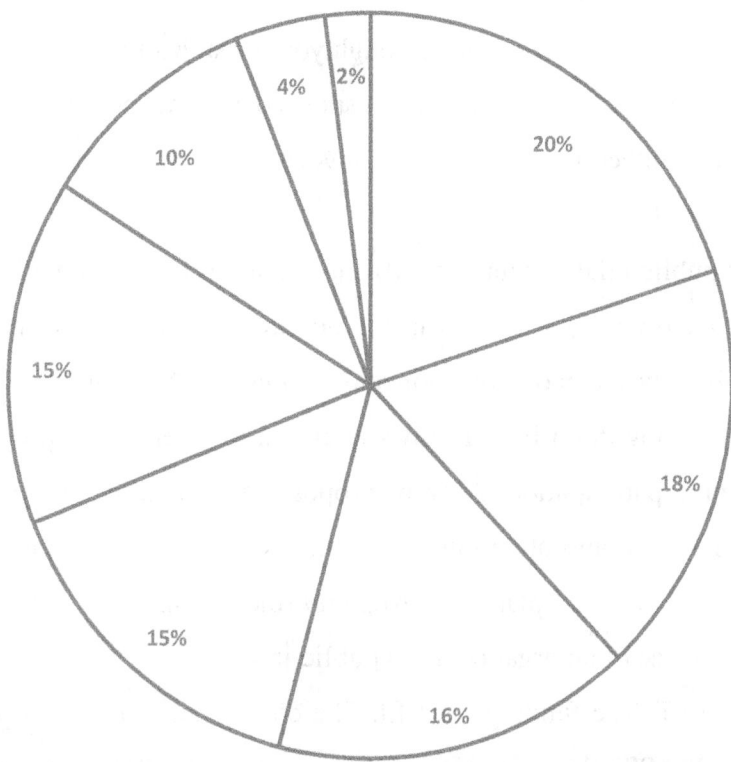

A grant proposal is a logical call to action. You are calling for the funder to act with you. As a blueprint for action, your grant proposal should explain the logical connections between your organization's intentions, capacity, and resources related to the funder's focus and guidelines while calling the funder to act upon your funding request, creating the foundation of a partnership. A call to action refers to any device designed to prompt an immediate response or encourage an instant collaboration. The device, in this case, is the grant proposal. (Please keep in mind that "immediate" is relative in that notice of a grant award could be up to six months or longer post-submission. Because most grant processes are deadline-driven for submission AND award decision, the response can be considered "immediate.") Grant funds are a facilitator to make positive change happen for a need in the community. Most change happens through partnerships. Even Bill Gates and Warren Buffet don't go it alone.

A grant is a demonstration of advocacy—for the grantee and grantor. Advocacy is related to partnering. Advocacy for your cause and mission is the act of pleading for, supporting, or recommending what you believe. Advocacy is an authentic, active espousal. You want to tell whoever will listen about the need and how it can be improved upon or eliminated in the community by advocacy through your organization's program/project. And because the pleas and recommendations are espoused in evidence of need and realistic expectations, they are authentic and worthy of advocacy by others. The grant application is one vehicle for espousal.

A grant is for public relations and advertising. Public relations and advertising are not entirely devoid of advocacy, particularly in the nonprofit world. Public relations involves promoting goodwill between an organization and the public, community, and customers (all stakeholders). Advertising describes or draws attention to a service or product in a public medium to encourage participation. A grant proposal does nothing if it does not proffer goodwill, and it certainly draws attention to a service or product requesting participation. A polished proposal for a well-planned program/project can also benefit as ongoing professional maintenance of an organization's public image.

A grant is SMART. The funding must fit. The components of a grant proposal and its award need to be SMART: Specific, Measurable, Achievable, Relevant, and Time-bound. SMART grant proposals emulate the following:

Specific—The program/project or other funding need is closely tied to the grantmaker's focus and guidelines.

Measurable—Qualitative and quantitative information about inputs, activities, outputs, outcomes, and impacts can be collected for the program/project needing funding.

Achievable—The expected outcomes and impacts support the mission and are realistic.

Relevant—The program/project or other funding need has an evidence-based design rooted in a need within the community.

Time-bound—The proposal delineates a period when the funded activities will occur.

What a grant is not –

I am sure you were inclined to answer the question, "What is a grant?" by simply saying that a grant is free money. As you can see from what a grant is, free money could not be further from the truth. A grant award is not free money. Sorry! Whether one or one of several, a grant award is not a quick solution for an organization's budget troubles. Understandably. Some organizations have grandiose ideas and well-intended energy. However, budgets and program/project specifics have to be realistic and ready to scale back some aspects to meet budget constraints and remain sustainable. Just because there is a grant funding opportunity that might relate to the mission or outcomes and impacts of a wish list for the future, it being awarded serves no purpose of solving real-time budget deficits. Creating a new program or project simply to qualify for a grant is a waste of time and energy, as there is no likely capacity for your organization to implement that new effort successfully. Suppose the new program/project cannot be implemented fully and completely. In that case, there is a risk of diminishing the credibility and reputation of the nonprofit and its stakeholders or imperiling the chances of future grant awards.

A grant award is not an easy and low-maintenance revenue stream. In addition to the many things that a grant can be for your organization, the process of finding, preparing, submitting, spending, and reporting on a grant award requires attention to detail, focus, persistence, creativity, human resources, payroll dollars, and the willingness to learn. These are all manageable, but you have to be aware of the commitment before managing it effectively.

A grant award is not free from incurred expenses. It is natural to think it is free since most grant funding does not come with a repayment schedule or interest rate. It is also natural to believe something that seems free should not incur costs to obtain. Wrong. Writing is daunting, and most people do not do it well. Formal business writing, which is precisely what a grant proposal encompasses, is more formidable than any other writing type. Most volunteers, board members, and staff are not good writers, nor do most people like to write (especially formal business writing). Although well-intended, the offer to have proposals written for free can end in disaster more times than not. The idea of getting grants written for free might seem like a good idea, but remember, free is often not FREE. While there is no invoice associated with a volunteer effort, a poorly executed attempt can result in not getting much-needed funding, diminished organization reputation, or eliminating the likelihood of being awarded money from that grantmaker in the future because of a less-than-competent submission. It can also result in damaging the relationship the organization has with that volunteer, board member, or staff. There is a risk of wasting time and delaying receiving funding because of missed deadlines, taking unnecessarily long periods writing and editing proposals, submitting proposals that were not thoroughly or adequately researched and vetted, or not being aware of other funding opportunities. Simply stated, most volunteers, board members, and staff do not grasp the grant proposal writing process.

A grant is not a way to fund or finance the start-up of a new nonprofit organization as seed money. That is not to say that new nonprofits cannot be awarded grants for traditional purposes.

The fundamental purpose of grant funding is the impact, not the money.

Funders have made the conscious decision to use their money, whether corporate or family wealth, to make a positive effect somewhere in the world. They might receive tax benefits or enjoy an ego-centric moment because of their giving, but those benefits would not come to fruition without making an impact with their money. More commonly than ever, many people and corporate entities are looking to align their financial aims with the ability to prompt change—to put their money to work in a way that will positively impact the world. The fundamental purpose of grant funding is the impact. Unless you are a great orator engaging vast audiences with mere words, you will need money to affect real change—the real change which is touted in your mission statement and explained through outputs, outcomes, and impacts in Program/Project Descriptions.

In an ideal world, the need would be minuscule or nonexistent. In the real world, factors such as the economy, health, and social issues make it necessary to prioritize financial resources. Funders and their benefactors collaborate with and prioritize the expectation that the results will translate into tangible benefits such as economic growth, health products, or solutions to social problems. Yes, the money awarded compensates salaries and fringe benefits, purchases supplies and equipment, pays overhead costs of the funded program or project, and more. However, these expenditures are what facilitate the impact.

People influence money decisions. Private and corporate foundations, along with government grant sources, are ultimately run by people. The grant funding decision-makers have to be convinced that the tangible benefits are not only possible but will be measurably achieved by the end of the funding period. The grant proposal convinces the funder that yours is the best program with the highest probability of success and impact.

Why should grant funding and management be SMART?

All planning, preparation, and grant reporting you do must be SMART: Specific, Measurable, Achievable, Relevant, and Time-bound. You need to work SMARTer, not harder. You need to write SMARTer, not harder. And by being SMART about your grants strategy, the grant proposals will do the work for you.

Why does a grant proposal need to be SMART? A grant proposal must be specific about what requires funding, including the type of funding and for what it will specifically pay. The milestones and results for grant funding should be measurable because the outputs and outcomes targeted in a grant application must include a metric (or metrics) with a target depicting what is considered a success. The grant criteria and proposal should align with the mission and activities in such a way to be achievable by setting challenging yet realistic expectations for outcomes and impacts. The relevancy of the funding request is demonstrated through the evidence-based need in the community and the impacts to be achieved by having enough funding to implement and complete the program/project. And finally, because grant funding is for a specific period, it is time-bound. The deadlines for submission and reporting related to grant funding also make it time-bound. (Metrics, outputs, outcomes, impacts, and community needs are explained in subsequent blocks.)

How grants for which you apply are vetted and selected should be just as focused, or SMART, as your organization's funding strategy is. Specific budgetary gaps and the nature of what requires funding should be identified. The parameters or guidelines offered by the grantmaker for the required funding must be quantified and assessed; in essence, measurable. Are the funds available and within the timeframe you need (i.e., achievable)? Are the funds available for the type of funding you need (program/project, capital, capacity-building, operations) and in the interest area your mission works to improve, such as poverty, disability inclusion, animal rescue, or food scarcity? In other words, are the funds and their criteria relevant to the organization's financial need? Do the grant proposal deadlines and award dates, if awarded, fit the timeframes required for your organization to make the program/project happen? And does the grant funding period provide intended and ample time to successfully carry out the activities for anticipated impacts?

Specific to grant activities, follow this template for a SMART Grants Strategy:

Specific—Provide a clear description of what needs to be achieved.

We need to secure grant funding for [purpose: name of program/project here].

Example: We need to secure grant funding for the Mentoring Individuals with Disabilities Flip It Reverse Job and Career Fair program.

Measurable—Include a metric with a target that indicates success.

We need to secure total grant funding in the amount of $___.__, representing [> 30%] of the total budget.

Example: We need to secure total grant funding in the amount of $4,458.00, representing 25% of the total $17,833 program budget.

Achievable—Set a challenging target but keep it realistic.

We need to identify gaps in the funding strategy and funding streams; identify only the purposes of grant funding that apply to the funding need(s).

Example: As of September 10, 2020, for the Flip It Reverse Job and Career Fair, there is a gap of $1,958 in secured grant funding. Additional grant funding (above 25% of the budget) for the program will allow us to redirect private donations and other funding streams within the organization.

Total grant funding required = $4,458—secured grant funding $2,500 = $1,958 gap

Relevant—Keep the outcomes and impacts consistent with high-level targets directly tied to the mission.

We need to ensure that the grant funding is available for the funding gaps in purpose, (time) period, and type for which you qualify.

Example: We need to secure at least $1,958 in grant funding for program-specific activities by December 31, 2020, from the foundation and corporate grant opportunities.

Time-bound—Set a date when your goal needs to be achieved.

We need to prioritize grant opportunities by date and amount, follow deadlines carefully, and make sure awards timeframes meet our grant funding requirements or wait until next/following year(s) to include it in your strategy.

Example: We need to prioritize grant opportunities by type, timeframe, and amount to determine strategy and identify additional opportunities if necessary for program implementation in the 2021 calendar year.

A grant proposal must be SMART because the mission, inputs, intended impacts, and related activities are SMART. You might not have known you were integrating a SMART goals strategy when the program/project was planned, but that is what skillful program planning does. And the more detailed it is, the better the chances for long-term sustainability and impact. (That is the point to all of this, isn't it?) It is essential to know the specific necessities regarding personnel, equipment, supplies, location(s), transportation, etc. From there, you will have an idea of the numbers. For example, from how many participants are anticipated or required and how success will be measured, it will be discerned whether or not the organization and community have the capacities to achieve implementation as well as the expected results (impacts). The research of need combined with the nonprofit's capacity determine that the program/project is relevant to the community. Although a program is a longer-reaching endeavor than a project, both are time-limited for completion.

A thought about communication style: Do not confuse a grant proposal with communications with donors or the general public. A proposal is not a monthly email blast, educational pamphlet, newsletter, or annual report. The proposal must show familiarity with the issue at hand with and focus on what will be done about the problem or need. Explain the problem, but then move on to how it will be addressed.

Understanding what a grant proposal is and can be is the best underpinning for grant proposal writing. Understanding that a grant is so much more than free money helps you know that the most assertive and most competitive grant applications seamlessly integrate compelling stories with facts and statistics. It puts into perspective that successful grant proposal writing presents thorough research and humanizes the material making your proposals stand out from the competition. It solidifies that a collaborative and transparent approach evolves by understanding that every organization has specific funding targets and is at various staffing and expertise stages, especially as these relate to grant proposal writing.

The Basics and Beyond

As we have determined, grants can play an integral role in implementing programs/projects and funding other needs while demonstrating sustainability and establishing credibility for the organization. Now we need to look at how this is possible. (I say program/project or funding need because not all grants are written for a program or project.) We need to look at the basics of grant funding and beyond before we get into writing and submitting the application. You will work SMARTer, not harder, once you understand the types of funders, types of funds available, various application processes and formats, and grant application components—the basics of grant proposal writing. You will also be able to work SMARTer by understanding the process beyond the application. This block will summarize parts and pieces of grants, and subsequent blocks will address their content.

The basics –

Let's break down the process from the beginning. The process tracks linear progress beginning with finding grantmakers through reporting on results when the funding period has ended. It is a management process outlined below and covered in greater detail in the "Grants Management" block. In addition to steps in the process, it is vital to understand the parts of the process. By parts, I mean types of funders, the structure of the funding, and types of grants. All three are distinct but related, and it is a hierarchy.

The process I propose includes six components, with some of those components having details specific to their role in the grant proposal writing process. The process involves grant funders, funding/funds, procedure, parts of the proposal, formats, and post-award activities. The grant funders' part of the process is broken into four types of funders. And the funding/funds part of the process is further defined by the various funding structures and types of grants—two different parts of funding.

Funders first: The type of grant you look for depends upon what you are funding, how quickly you need to know if that grant has been awarded, how much time you have to dedicate to completing a grant application, how much the ask will be, and your organization's capacity to manage specific grants. There is a limited number of types of grant funders. These include government, corporate giving, community and civic organizations, and foundations. (Remember, we are only talking about grant funders, not individual or other corporate funding such as sponsorships. There are many different funding streams and opportunities for nonprofits besides grants.) Grants for for-profit businesses and individuals are typically funded through government and foundation grants.

Government funders include federal, state, county, and municipality (city). The most common government grants are awarded from federal and state government agencies. Government grants are the most time-consuming because they are the most labor-intensive for which to apply, but they can and often offer the most funds. Corporate funding can be in the form of money or in-kind products or services.

Please note that not all corporations with a corporate giving program have formed a foundation from which to distribute funds. Corporate giving and corporate foundations are prevalent. The average notification time from the submission deadline date is no more than 90 days. There is plenty of information on whom they support, types of programs/projects in their focus areas, the average amount awarded, and more. This information can be beneficial when fine-tuning applications for these grantmakers as well as developing a strategic grant plan.

Community or civic organizations refer to a community-based company, club, committee, association, corporation, or any other group of people acting together voluntarily. They are primarily established to advance educational, charitable, religious, cultural, or local economic development purposes. For example, the local Rotary Club may have its own foundation that provides local grant opportunities. Public and community foundations require a little more relationship building than government or corporate ones. Sometimes, the bigger and better your branding helps secure community foundation money. By branding, I mean your board member affiliations and other funding partners.

Foundations include corporate, family, and other private entities, which can be independent, community, national, and research organizations. Foundations vary broadly in size, size of awards, simplicity or complexity, and requisite for establishing a relationship. Private and family foundations are often more easily accessible; they have lower-average awards but are usually more flexible in their criteria.

Funding and funds next: There are four structures of funding: Competitive, formula, continuation, and pass-through. The typical nonprofit is not too concerned about what structure of funding a grant will be. However, it is essential to know the structures to understand the process from beginning to end. Competitive funding, also known as discretionary funding, is a process of proposal selection based on the evaluation by a reviewer or team of reviewers. Funding is based on the merits of the application, and recipients are not pre-determined. This type of funding is the most common for many nonprofits. Many for-profit and arts/writers grants are discretionary as well.

In contrast to competitive funding, formula grants are given to pre-determined recipients. Non-competitive awards are usually allocated to eligible entities according to population and/or other census criteria, and all applicants who meet the minimum requirements of the application process are entitled to receive money. State and federal government grants, as well as academic grants, are frequently this structure of funding.

Continuation funding grants offer current award recipients the option of renewing grants for the following funding period (usually one year—fiscal or calendar). Some of these grants are restricted to existing grantees, while others invite submissions from current grantees and new applicants for the next funding cycle. Since priority is often given to continuing applicants, consider entering into a partnership with a currently funded entity if you are a new applicant. Larger organizations apply for more continuation funding than smaller and start-up ones do. Organizational capacity impacts its ability to apply and manage continuation funding.

Pass-through grants are funds given by the federal government to the states for further distribution to local governments. Under this funding structure, states may disburse federal funds to eligible local jurisdictions through formula allocations or open competitions. Occasionally, tax-exempt organizations might receive a government grant to distribute to nonprofits meeting strict criteria. This became more common in the United States during the first few months of the Corona Virus pandemic in 2020 and 2021 to get funds allocated to social services and other causes more quickly. Pass-through funding is also allocated in a fiduciary agent business model.

The four structures of funding awarded by a funder are done via a variety of types of grants. What I mean by types of grants is what they can be used for—their purpose. The purpose, or how the money can be spent, is found in the terms or keywords identified in the grantmaker's guidelines. Purposes include program/project, capital, capacity building, (general) operating, and research. Matching and challenge are two other guidelines that a funder can set. The funder focus or funding guidelines explain the purpose for which the grant is awarded. For example, for a grant award benefitting a program called Flip It Reverse Job and Career Fair, the funder's focus could be workforce development for people with disabilities and could stipulate that the money can be spent only for the program-related expenses, no indirect operating costs or building renovation. As another example, a different funder with the same focus might have guidelines that stipulate that the money can be spent on any of the organization's budget items. The most common grant funding for nonprofits is direct program/project expenses. Conversely, grants for a for-profit business can be used for anything related to why the business applies for the award, such as start-up, research, inventory, or technology. Grants for individuals, including artists and writers, are usually quite specific about the intended use of the money.

Let's look at what each of these purposes (generally) include:

Program/project funding supports specific programs or projects for a pre-determined period. This is the money required to pay for the inputs (resources) to execute the activities necessary for program/project implementation.

Capital-building grants can be a part of capital campaigns so that funders can provide large-scale grants to help nonprofits realize their plans of purchasing a building or land, renovating, or buying a large piece of equipment, all of which are examples of capital expenditures. These grants are typically reserved for established nonprofits or nonprofits with deep connections, relationships, or proof of impact.

Capacity-building grants help organizations increase their ability to do more in a particular area of interest. These grants are for a process rather than a program/project. For example, a small nonprofit might receive a capacity-building grant to help it increase its fundraising capacity by purchasing donor management software or hiring a professional fundraiser.

Operating fund grants give ongoing support to an organization. They help with operating expenses, direct and indirect. These are highly sought but hard to find. Small, family foundations are more likely to provide operating fund grants than larger, well-known foundations. General operating grants are unrestricted funds that enable an organization to carry out its mission. Funding awards are intended to underwrite an organization's administrative and infrastructure costs, assist with strategic financial and organizational capacity, and/or help maintain core programs/projects and essential staff.

Research grants are typically found in academia and research-oriented nonprofits. In academic settings, they are often attached to a particular faculty member and go where they go. Research grants are awarded for conducting research as the program/project or the organization's primary activity, not for doing research to develop a needs statement or program/project description.

Matching grants are an effective means of funding small projects, especially those with active community support. A matching grant is intended to encourage and incentivize community members to donate to an organization. It requires a specified amount of funds raised from other sources on a dollar-for-dollar basis or another stated matching criterion.

Challenge grants are similar to Matching Grants. Challenge grants are donations made by a grant-making organization to a nonprofit organization once that institution has raised a certain amount of funds as described by the challenge, which sounds very much like the Matching grant. In some cases, usually more creative than a typical grant proposal or mail campaign, the Challenge grant is based on an activity or quantified level of participation, for example, instead of a monetary match. The challenge is usually fiscally based.

A sixth type of funding, not mentioned in the original list, is everything else. There are other types of grant funding not related to nonprofits, such as for-profit businesses, start-up money for for-profit entities, artists and writers, incentives, personal development, and education grants. The same general concepts for grant proposal writing apply when applying for these grants. Here are a few examples:

- Grants for a researcher to complete their dissertation
- Grants for homeowners to collect rainwater at their residence
- Grants for small business owners to develop or expand their businesses
- Grants for writers and artists for a specific creative endeavor or general support

Based on these explanations, questions about what expenses can be included in which type of grant asks probably arise. It takes some degree of logic as well as practice and even a little educated guessing! The blocks on "Program/Project Descriptions," "Budgets," and "Logic Models" offer much detail about estimating and making the correct ask for expenditures in the proposal.

The expenses on which the grant money is spent are restricted or unrestricted. (Remember, the things that grant money can be used for are not the same as the type of funding or the type of grant, as discussed in the previous paragraphs.) Restricted funds are designated or "restricted" to a particular purpose, usually a specific program/project. An example from our sample program is if the grant money could only be used for soft skills training for job development for people with disabilities. As an additional example, the grant restrictions might require no payroll expenses can be funded.

Unrestricted funds are contributions the nonprofit may use for any purpose. The nonprofit can choose how to use that money and usually allows operating expenses, including payroll and fringe benefits, in those choices. There are circumstances when a grantmaker awards unrestricted funds to one program/project. This would mean that the money could be spent on anything supporting the designated program/project, not anything within the organization. Only the funder can stipulate if an award is restricted or unrestricted. Most grantmakers make it clear whether or not the funds have restrictions in their criteria.

There are good reasons to be completely clear about how the organization plans to use the gift when submitting a grant proposal. There is an ethical obligation to honor a grantor's guidelines and intentions, and there are legal responsibilities too. If a grantmaker restricts a donation to a particular purpose and the nonprofit does not comply, the grantmaker can demand a refund. The grantor can take legal action, if needed, and report the nonprofit to the Office of the Attorney General in the state in which the nonprofit operates. Whether the grant money is restricted or unrestricted should be a consideration when considering applying for that money.

This is an excellent place to point out that the purposes of grant funding are entirely unrelated to the parts of the organization's funding strategy. (Funding strategy is discussed in the block on "What Is a Grant?") Each piece of the funding strategy is a component of operations and governance. The inputs and activities to implement these components require funding. This is an important distinction that you want to communicate accurately and briefly with the grant funder.

Now that the types of funders, funding, and purposes of grant money are understood, understanding the procedures for getting that money is crucial. There are procedures to find and vet grant opportunities, build relationships with (some) grantmakers, and subsequently complete and submit proposals. All of which are a part of the grant proposal writer's responsibility.

The next step in the process is that procedure for finding the money and finding where the money might come from or from whom is a process. For now, understanding that there are resources at-the-ready to be mined and resources that take a little time and trouble to find is key. Just as a winning lottery ticket does not merely show up in your mailbox, grant money does not magically appear on the balance sheet. There is an effort required and some strategy to find it. The parts of the finding and vetting process that should be mastered include the ready resources for finding grants, being observant and creative when identifying additional grant opportunities, prioritizing, and tracking. The entire process is thoroughly detailed in the "Finding and Vetting Grants" block.

Building relationships with (some) grant funders is a balancing act within the process. Relationship building is mutual and purposeful. It is not simply a social media post or follow, nor is it entreating. It is not transactional. Local and regional funders, including government agencies, are the most receptive to relationship building. They want to know the community leaders and be engaged with their activities and missions. Reciprocally, you want to be tuned into them. There is a balance between being intentional and being too evasive. A few suggested means of engagement include following social media accounts, subscribing to their newsletter, or inviting them for a visit or coffee. Engagement might also include directly asking what is important to them in their partnerships. Do not force the fit, however. Most importantly, conduct the relationship-building independently and well in advance of a grant submission timeline. If a proposal is declined, use that as an opportunity to initiate a more aligned relationship.

A note about contacting the funder before or immediately after submission. If there is no established relationship, should you? The answer is, "It depends upon the funder." It is okay to contact them to clarify something on the application in most cases. You do not want to contact the funder to tout your program/project or organization. If you try to be clever and turn the call into that, it will do more harm than good.

Before cogently completing a grant proposal, you need to know how you will be asking for the financial partnership. There is a process of how a proposal is submitted. In most instances, the submission process is one step—completing a questionnaire or formatted proposal form. Most of these one-step asks are completed online or through email submission. (Please note that creating an account on the funder's online platform does not count as a separate step.) However, some grantmakers want to streamline their review process by "auditioning" the program/project without a full proposal. This is usually done through a Letter of Intent or Letter of Inquiry (LOI), a response to a Request for Proposal (RFP), an eligibility quiz, or an email briefly explaining the need or program/project (an informal LOI). The title Letter of Introduction is interchangable with Letter of Intent or Letter of Inquiry. From these "auditions," the grantmaker will select a group of programs/projects or organizations for full proposal or application submissions. (The parts of the application are detailed in the next section.)

This is an excellent place to explain solicited and unsolicited applications. Some grantmakers have very targeted agendas. Some will indicate they do not or are not accepting unsolicited proposals—a polite way for them to say, "If you don't have an invitation to the party, you cannot RSVP." Unless the organization has a direct and viable connection to that grantmaker, who is only accepting solicited proposals, move on. Perhaps include them on a list to build a relationship, but it is not worth the time to go after this grant more often than not.

Before you sit down to write the proposal itself, determine the style of the form being completed. Can you access the form and save it as a word document (or another fillable document) to work on at your pace and with your team? When you start filling in the lines or boxes, can the content be saved to come back to later, or do you need to complete the form and submit it in one sitting? Are you aware of the character or word count restrictions, if any? Suppose the structure or formatting is left up to you—do you have a comprehensive template that provides information in a logical, expected order?

To work SMARTer, not harder, prioritize the opportunities found. There is no singular formula for doing this because every nonprofit has distinct priorities. To rank the opportunities, asampling of your organization's considerations includes the submission deadline, the decision timeframe, the amount (will it help enough), the reporting requirements, and how closely aligned the mission is to the funder focus. A logical grant-ready order to rank potential submissions is the alignment, timing considerations, amount, and reporting requirements. SMART grant readiness looks like this:

Specific—The organization has identified all the ways in which grant funding will benefit programs/projects and other areas of the nonprofit to help it accomplish the mission. The organization has identified all the information about the programs/projects and all operations required by grantmakers.

Measurable—Funding gaps related to grants have been calculated.

Achievable—The nonprofit has assessed its position regarding its ability to submit successful grant applications.

Relevant—The organization has adopted the mindset that grants require experience and diligence to execute the tasks in this area successfully.

Time-bound—The grant proposal writer and team accept that the grant process must be ongoing while meeting deadlines to achieve outcomes and impacts.

Now that grant opportunities have been identified and prioritized, and general expectations are known, you need to be aware of what information a grantmaker will likely request. Not every part of the following compendium will be requested in every proposal. However, knowing the full scope required for the most rigorous applications will prevent stressful surprises later.

This seemingly formidable list of documents and information is less daunting when delineated by the likelihood of being required. Many templates or samples for these documents are available on the SMART Money Grant Writing website or by request. The information that you can rely on being required in most grant proposals includes:

- Organization and contact information
- Mission Statement
- Needs Statement
- Program/Project Description
- Evaluation Method(s)
- Budget with a budget narrative for the organization and/or program/project
- Key Staff and Board of Directors list, bios
- Additional funding sources
- Collaborations and partnerships, including in-kind
- Letter of Nonprofit Status Determination from the IRS

The information that sometimes is requested or might be optional to incorporate includes:

- Cover Letter or Cover Sheet
- Executive Summary
- Letters of Support
- Letters of Agreement, Memorandums of Agreement
- Sustainability Statement

- Conflict of Interest policy
- Diversity, Equity, Inclusion, and Access (DEIA) policy
- Other policies—Nondiscrimination Policy, Technology Use Policy, Financial Management Policies,
- Annual report
- Audited Annual Financial Report or Copies of Policies and Procedures accepted in lieu of Audited Financials (Please refer to the block on "Financials")
- Financial Statements Balance Sheet
- W-9
- Unique Entity Identifier (UEI), formerly the DUNS number
- Purpose Statement of organization
- Purpose Statement of the grant application
- Volunteer hours
- Marketing Media coverage
- Sponsor packets
- Testimonials
- Video(s)

A word about purpose statements: This is the part, when required, where many mistakes are made because of misinterpretation. There are two very different purpose statements: 1) the purpose of the organization and 2) the purpose of the grant proposal; ensure for which is being asked.

If you think the list of what might be required for a proposal is formidable, proposal formats can be just as formidable, not to mention frustrating—online, word or character counts, free form, fax, or mail paper applications. Most grant applications are submitted online; the occasional request to mail or fax still exists. Some applications or Letters of Intent can be emailed to the funder, but only if that is their instruction or request. A feeling of exhilaration will overcome you when you come across a free-form online form with no word or character restrictions! As a grant proposal writer, you aspire to be a wordsmith flawlessly connecting mission to needs with program/project descriptions and budget narratives. In actuality, you become a word-counting smith.

There are many online formats for grant submission. A few will have no option to save and return later. With these, you need to be prepared to complete the proposal's content in one sitting or enter the information multiple times from the start, wasting time and conjuring frustration. Some forms can be started, saved, and continued later. These are ideal. Working from your desktop or laptop at your discretion is even more ideal. Whenever possible, save the blank form as a Word document to work at your leisure. A screenshot might serve the same purpose of writing the content of each section at your pace and avoiding submitting accidentally before the proposal is completed and polished. Working on a Word document on your desktop is appreciably easier than getting timed out online or the power going out in the middle of the unsaved or unsavable application. Whether working at your pace or online, save the application frequently; make this a part of your grant proposal writing process.

Another valuable practice for the grant proposal writing process is streamlining the content writing procedure. When a section of a proposal is written with word or character restrictions (for example, restricted to 500 words), save it. Save it for the next time a similar restriction is invoked. Why reinvent the wheel? Create a document specifically for content and information already accommodating constraints. Copy and paste that content into this master word/character count document, notating or labeling the specific restriction and section: "Needs Statement 300 characters," "Flip It Reverse Job and Career Fair Description 500 words."

Remember, no two grant applications are ever the same. The parts of grant applications can vary in the order of requested information, character or word counts of content or responses, the detail required, the scope of financial information, and more. Typically, the higher the ask, the more information will be required. The more money a funder is willing to commit, the more they want to see well-thought-out and evidence-based programs/projects, all-encompassing evaluation methods, fiscal responsibility, and evidence of sustainability. Government grants are usually the most time-consuming, requiring the most detailed information, reporting, and accountability. Grants applications for for-profit businesses and individuals have similar variables and are similarly scalable to nonprofit applications.

In grant proposal writing, most of our time is spent writing from scratch because we think it is easier and we know the content so well. This opens up much longer editing time and the potential for omissions and mistakes. Take a minute when vetting a grant opportunity, adding it to the Grants Tracker, or when beginning to write the proposal to note which documents and attachments are required and which ones are optional. Start gathering those that are not in the shared file early on. Last-minute surprises will cause, at minimum, frustration and, at most, not being able to apply. Streamlining the grant proposal writing process through your content is not only common sense but also results-driven. It is SMART.

Another way to streamline the grant proposal writing process is only to write the content necessary for a particular application that cannot be copied and pasted from content already created. What I mean is that some proposal content will change from application to application, while other content will remain the same for an entire fiscal or calendar year and perhaps longer. Why would information change?: To conform with the character or word counts, to focus on the grant's funding priority or guidelines, to emphasize a specific aspect of the program/project, info may not be required, and no two applications are identical.

We know why content might change. Let's look at when it will never change, sometimes change, or always change from application to application.

Information and content that never* change:
- Organization's history and contact information (legal name, d/b/a name, address, phone, fax, website, general/info@ email)
- Staff and Board of Directors lists with bios; advisory board(s)
- Budget(s) and budget narrative(s)
- Year-end Financial Info—Balance Sheet, Financial Statements, Annual audit

or summary

- Executive Summaries

(*Never, in this case, means almost never. Information in any of this content or these documents could change during a fiscal or calendar year if, for example, staff or board members change or if significant modifications to budgets occur. This content would be updated, not changed.)

Information and content that always change from application to application:

- Cover Sheet, Cover Letter
- Attachments—IRS Letter of Determination, Conflict of Interest Policy, Nondiscrimination Policy, Technology Use Policy, Budgets, Financial Documents, Diversity, Equity and Inclusion Policy, List of Collaborations (program/project partners, sponsors, donations, in-kind contributions) including volunteer hours, Marketing collateral (Brochures, FAQs, media, press releases, website),
- Lists of inventories (capacity building, unrestricted, operating grants), Letters of Support, Testimonials, and Award Letters
- The order in which the information and content are presented or organized

No two applications are the same. Therefore, some information and content might be different from proposal to proposal. A Cover Sheet or Cover Letter should always be included. The attachments always change. Most commonly required ones include the IRS Letter of Determination, budget and financial information, and a list of collaborations and partners. Notice I say the documents change; content in these documents never changes (although they can be updated in some cases). The other content-related piece that reliably changes from proposal to proposal is the order in which the various components are organized. I sometimes think there is a conspiracy to see how much grant makers collectively can challenge us!

Information and content that can change from application to application:

- Program/Project Descriptions
- Needs Statements

- Purpose Statements
- Financial information
- Program/Project Evaluations

The stuff that can change, from proposal to proposal, usually involves character or word count restrictions. The Program/Project Descriptions, Needs Statements, Purpose Statements, and Program/Project Evaluations are often edited to make them fit. Additionally, it seems that every grantmaker has its ideas on financial and budget requirements. Some want just the program budget. Some want the program budget with a narrative. Some want the program/project and organization budgets, and financial statements from the beginning of time. The budget narrative might have to be edited to meet word or character counts, too. Note, however, that the content and numbers of the budgets never change (unless needing to be updated); just the particular documents representing the budget vary from grant to grant.

Be mindful that once an online application is submitted, it usually cannot be changed or updated. Ensure you have saved a copy of or printed the proposal before clicking submit. You want to know what was submitted exactly to each grantmaker for clarification to staff or board of directors or if the grantmaker asks you to revise or clarify the submitted ask.

Award declines or rejections are a part of the grant process as well. It is estimated that less than 20% of asks are awarded. The reasons are as varied as the number of asks. When a decline to fund is received, cordially inquire why. A great way to continue forging a relationship with the grantmaker and open the door to re-submit at a later date is to inquire, "How can Mentoring Individuals with Disabilities strengthen the likelihood of funding from the Weisenberger Family Foundation in the future?" Blurting out, "Why didn't we get the money?" is not the best approach, although it may feel like the right one at that moment.

The process, or grant cycle, concludes with the post-award management. The criteria or guidelines will often summarize the funder's expectations and requirements for assurance their money was spent as intended and promised. By applying for and accepting a grant award, remember, you are entering into a formal, binding agreement. Post-award management begins when the money is accepted (i.e., deposited into the organization's bank account). Everyone must account for the funds, from the Executive Director responsible for all operations to the employee making purchases for the funded program to all internal and external stakeholders. The funder often requires formal reporting at the end of the grant period; some require periodic, deadline-driven reporting too.

Beyond the basics –

If you are starting or started a nonprofit thinking that grant money is going to pay a keen salary or allow you to take the easy path away from your current dreadful job, you are sadly mistaken. You can earn a competitive salary and work on the desired mission, and grant money can help make that happen, but only if the planning is strategic and purposeful. Too often, nonprofits think grants are the solution to all opportunities and threats to the organization. They may believe grants will help a nonprofit get started, save it from going under, or meet next month's bills. These misnomers arise because there is a sizeable misunderstanding about the basics of how nonprofits are funded and the essential role that grants should play in that funding.

A robust grants strategy always has a list of opportunities with varying deadlines and award amounts. Grant A will typically be awarded once, with no renewal opportunity. Grant B should have similar criteria to Grant A, sort of a replacement the following year. A robust strategy also includes an assortment of possibilities that represent all gaps in funding throughout the organization. Nonprofits that are the most successful in getting grants have designated someone who is always looking for grant opportunities, and there is a dedicated staff or contractor to write, monitor, and report back to the foundations.

Here are some of the realities about grants that every nonprofit must understand to put them in perspective. Ensure a well-balanced strategy of revenue streams is developed to sustain the organization for the years ahead, in which grants can be a part. Here are a few realities to think about:

The majority of grants rarely fund operating costs. It is less common for a grantmaker to provide money to keep your organization's doors open—operating expenses such as rent/mortgage, utilities, salaries, and fringe benefits. Grants are usually intended to fill the gap between 100% funded and money in other funding strategy streams. Grants work well to help create a new program or grow an existing one. However, they are not meant to sustain an organization or even a particular program/project. Grant applications ferret out plans for continuing the program/project for the long term. Grants are meant to be short-term infusions of money to achieve a particular purpose and fill a reasonable funding gap. Demonstrating how other parts of the monetary funding strategy will combine with collaborations and in-kind partnerships to implement the program/project to achieve anticipated results is extremely helpful when asking for grant funds.

It is important to note that as this book is published, more and more funders realize programs/projects implemented by even the most sustainable entities have operating costs associated with the program/project. They are allowing for some operating expenses in their awards criteria. Some operating expenses can be prorated and included in the funding for a specific program/project; how this is done is covered in subsequent blocks.

Grants are a small part of any organization's funding strategy. A nonprofit industry best practice is that no more than 30% of the funding strategy should be from grants. Separately, the majority of grants are awarded for a finite period—usually 12 months. Some awards are multi-year funding and typically stipulate portions of the total funding for each year of the award. Because there are fewer guarantees about grant funding than alternative revenues, a multi-pronged and strategic funding scheme is necessary to remain sustainable.

The grant process takes a long time. You cannot expect to get a grant quickly or instantly. It takes time to find the appropriate grant opportunity that is most likely to fund the program/project. It takes time to develop the proposal, and it takes more time after that for it to be accepted or rejected. Even with the rare instance that a volunteer or board member has a family foundation guaranteed to write a check, it takes time. If a nonprofit is financially unstable, going after grants will not help in the long run.

Grants can be very specific about how the award is spent. Earlier, you learned about the purposes of funding. The purposes can be limiting as well as the criteria and funder's focus. Many grants have conditions and restrictions. They are meant to address a particular problem, and funds must be spent strictly on that program or project. There are reporting requirements and oversight. Sometimes, foundation grants specify the nonprofit to find additional money to match the grant before it is awarded.

Procuring a grant takes time and resources. No two grant applications are alike. It takes time to complete each application effectively. That time is part of the human resources required to procure grant funding. Whether a paid, experienced grant proposal writer is on staff or contracted, someone must spend time writing the proposal.

Grant funding is not required for sustainability. Indeed, grants are available to be a part of any nonprofit's funding strategy. However, grants are not required to make a program/project successful or an organization sustainable, but it is essential to keep perspective.

A word about grant fraud: Fraudulent behavior can take the form of embezzlement, theft, bribery, or false claims and statements. Grant fraud typically occurs when award recipients attempt to deceive the funder about their spending of award money. Besides triggering lost efficiency and waste of funders' monies, grant fraud can also significantly impact entities found to have carried it out. Consequences can include debarment from receiving future funding, administrative recoveries of funds, civil lawsuits, and criminal prosecution in local, state, and federal jurisdictions.

A word about grant scams: The allure of so-called "free money" has enabled scam artists to prey on people's hopes by promising access to grants, often for a fee. No legitimate grant funding requires an application fee for nonprofits. (Well, almost no legitimate grant has a fee. On rare occasions, a funder might charge a nominal fee to apply. This is usually for artists' and writers' grants, though, and is, on average, $10-25 to cover administrative costs of reviewing the applications.) Keep in mind, too, federal grants are rarely awarded to individuals seeking personal benefits, and grant scams occur at a much higher rate for those touted as "individual." Business grant scams also happen more frequently than nonprofit ones.

A strategy must be devised to accommodate these realities. The word strategy, which has crept into our grant discussion, might be a new idea for you when you think about grants for nonprofit funding. A strategy is a plan of action or policy designed to achieve a primary or overall aim. Ask 100 nonprofit professionals about strategy, and you will muddle through

100 different answers. Developing an effective strategy takes experience and is definitely beyond the basics of typical nonprofit job descriptions. Being strategic is smart and capable. We can narrow the seemingly endless versions of strategy to SMART. While SMART goals (Specific, Measurable, Achievable, Relevant, and Time-bound) are not a new or unheard-of idea, applying the SMART strategy to nonprofit activities, particularly grant activities, might be.

The following is how the SMART acronym is best applied to grant proposal writing:

Specific—Provide a clear description of what is expected to be achieved.

Measurable—Include a metric with a target that indicates success.

Achievable—Set a challenging target but keep it realistic.

Relevant—Keep the outcomes and impacts consistent with high-level targets directly tied to the mission.

Time-bound—Set a date when your target is expected to be achieved.

Specific to grant activities, follow this template for a SMART Grants Strategy:

Specific—Provide a clear description of what is expected to be achieved.

We need to secure grant funding for [purpose: name of program/project here].

Example: We need to secure grant funding for the Mentoring Individuals with Disabilities Flip It Reverse Job and Career Fair program.

Measurable—Include a metric with a target that indicates success.

We need to secure total grant funding in the amount of $___.___, [> 30%] of the total budget.

Example: We need to secure total grant funding in the amount of $4,458.00, representing 25% of the total $17,833 program budget.

Achievable—Set a challenging target but keep it realistic.

We need to identify gaps in the funding strategy and funding streams; identify only the purposes of grant funding that apply to the funding gap(s).

Example: As of September 10, 2020, for the Flip It Reverse Job and Career Fair, there is a gap of $1,958 in secured grant funding. Additional grant funding (above 25% of the budget) for the program will allow us to redirect private donations and other funding streams within the organization.

Total grant funding required = $4,458 - secured grant funding $2,500 = $1.958 gap

Relevant—Keep the outcomes and impacts consistent with high-level targets directly tied to the mission.

We need to ensure that the grant funding is available for the funding gaps in purpose, (time) period, and type for which you qualify.

Example: We need to secure at least $1,958 in grant funding for program-specific activities by December 31, 2020, from the foundation and corporate grant opportunities.

Time-bound—Set a date when your target is expected to be achieved.

We need to prioritize grant opportunities by date and amount, follow deadlines carefully, and make sure awards timeframes meet our grant funding requirements or wait until next/following year(s) to include it in your strategy.

Example: We need to prioritize grant opportunities by type, timeframe, and amount to determine strategy and identify additional opportunities if necessary for program implementation in the 2022 calendar year.

Since we set forth some realities, let's dispel some myths.

Myth: *Grant funds are not awarded to new or small nonprofits.* I offer a rare anecdote: The first grant proposal I wrote was my first awarded grant. I applied before receiving the Letter of Determination from the IRS Charitable Division. The program was evidence-based, the needs research was current and cited, the budget was thorough and realistic, and the content was proofed and edited for clarity and polish. The ask was $5,000; the award was $10,000. True story.

Myth: *A grant is never awarded a second time.* Many grant types are awarded more than once to the same organization to support the same or different programs/projects. Building a relationship with the funder is crucial to making this happen. Equally critical is timely, comprehensive, and valid reporting of how the funder's money was used per their reporting requirements, agreed to when submitting the application and accepting the money.

Myth: *Foundations cut back on funding in tough times.* Those engaged in serving the greater good, regardless of the role, tend to step up in times of strife. One example is that in 2017, as a possible response to the government cuts to social service funding and personal tax exemption restructuring, grant money increased by 6%. Do not be dispirited by ups and downs. Foundations also increased giving during the Corona Virus pandemic in 2020 and 2021.

Myth: *Grants do not fund operating costs.* Just as we said that many grants do not fund operating expenses, it is a myth that none do. Operations can be funded wholly or in part. Narrow the grant opportunity search to operations focuses or target results on grants that will support operations or non-program/project gaps. Look closely at funder guidelines and the budget to identify parts of operations that can legitimately be included in the ask. They exist more frequently than you think.

Myth: *My nonprofit does not have the capacity to write grant proposals.* That is the exact reason why you are reading this book. Capacity is only limited by creativity—creativity in carving time, learning best practices, and honing skills utilizing shortcuts others do not know about and have not trained.

Myth: *No relationship with the foundation means no money.* If you are limiting the opportunities to only foundations or other grantmakers familiar with your organization or program/project, much funding might never materialize. There are many, many grantmakers wanting to fund viable missions, regardless of the geography or notoriety. (Do not confuse notoriety with credibility and authority. Every credible authority started somewhere, without high public awareness.)

Myth: *An organization must have tax-exempt status to apply.* It is not a myth that most grant funding is awarded to organizations with tax-exempt status. However, there are grants for for-profit endeavors and individuals. There are also nonprofit business models that replicate tax-exempt status without holding their own Letter of Determination. The program/project can partner with an established 501(c)3 to share the funding.

A fiduciary agent or fiscal sponsor is also an option. In this case, a fiduciary agent provides legitimacy and oversight to the program/project or organization's grant money. A legal agreement permits using the fiduciary agent's 501(c)3 status to secure grant money, use it prudently, and report as required. Typically, the fiduciary agent receives the money for allocation to the partnered organization. A fiduciary agent or fiscal sponsor should only be engaged if they AND you (the recipient-to-be of the pass-through money/grant funding) are keenly familiar with the responsibilities and rights regarding this type of business partnership.

This list of myths is not all-inclusive but should dispel the angst of the most prolific ones.

Writing is only a small part of developing a grant proposal, and it is only important as a vehicle for clearly articulating the problem, the plan, and the intended results. Clear writing cannot disguise a muddled understanding of the problem or an illogical plan of action. Dramatic writing might initially catch the reader's attention, but it cannot support an argument that does not coalesce. Understanding the basics of grant proposal writing and beyond will coalesce all the parts of the process. And by the way, you are a grant proposal writer, not a grant writer. A grant writer, technically speaking, is the one who writes the grant criteria or guidelines and designs the proposal.

Getting Grant-Ready

Being grant-ready is a mindset. There is work to get grant-ready. Work beyond that Letter of Determination from the IRS. Work beyond lively, productive conversations about programs and missions during staff and board meetings. It is work to pull together the documents and information required in grant applications. It is work figuring out which materials are ready to go and which content has to be written. It can be daunting.

Being grant-ready is more than checking a few boxes on a list of suggested documents or having 501(c)3 tax-exempt status in hopes of winning grant funding. A grant-ready mindset is more important than having an electronic folder of attachable-ready files. Funding is the lifeblood of any organization. I know you think the lifeblood is the mission and commitment of staff and volunteers. However, the mission is lost without funding, and the commitment is not sustainable.

I have found that small- to medium-sized and start-up nonprofit organizations want the (grant) money but are often not in the mindset to do what is most necessary to get the (grant) money. Here is what I have found these organizations erroneously believe:

- A volunteer, board member, or staff member can write a grant proposal effectively.
- A grant proposal is written in a couple of hours.
- The going rate for grant proposal writing is $12 an hour.
- Necessary information for most grant proposals is ready because they have marketing collateral or a business plan.
- An organization should not spend money to get (grant) money.

Whether you want to submit a funding request to local foundations or globally recognized corporate foundations, you need to be ready to present your best effort. It is natural to think it is free since most grant funding does not come with a repayment schedule or interest rate. It is also natural to think that something free should not incur costs to obtain.

Wrong. Writing is daunting, and most people do not do it well. Formal business writing, which is precisely what a grant proposal encompasses, is more daunting than any other writing type. Most volunteers, board members, and staff are not good writers, nor do most like writing, especially formal business writing.

Although well-intended, an offer to write proposals for free for your organization can end in disaster more times than not. The idea of getting grants written for free might seem like a good idea, but remember, free is often not FREE. While there is no invoice associated with a volunteer effort, a poorly executed attempt can result in not getting much-needed funding, diminished organization reputation, or eliminating the likelihood of being awarded money from that grantmaker in the future because of a less-than-competent submission leaving a lasting unfavorable impression. It can also result in damaging the relationship the organization has with that volunteer, board member, or staff. There is also a risk of wasting time and delaying receiving funding because of missing deadlines, unnecessarily long periods of writing and editing proposals, submitting proposals that were not thoroughly researched and vetted, or not being aware of other funding opportunities. Simply stated, most volunteers, board members, and staff do not know the grant proposal writing process.

The first step to being a grant-ready organization is to accept the fact that an experienced grant proposal writer is necessary. Recognizing that fact includes understanding that there is a monetary value to using someone with proven experience and, therefore, an expense. Understanding these value and expense components progresses the acceptance that it will take money to get (grant) money. Grant proposal writing must be included in the organization's budget, not as an in-kind donation line item or included in volunteer hours. This requires a grant-ready mindset.

Once your mindset is grant-ready, you can start gathering the documents and information required for results-driven, well-written, and awarded grant proposals. There is a process involved in preparing to complete grant applications, and there are things to consider for how well-positioned the organization is to be awarded grant money. These are two completely separate activities. Funding is competitive. Be ready for competition by understanding the process and considering your current position. Here is the SMART way to get grant-ready:

Specific—The organization has identified all of the ways in which grant funding will benefit programs/projects and other areas of the nonprofit to help it accomplish the mission. Additionally, the organization has identified all the information about the programs/projects and all operations required by grantmakers.

Measurable—Funding gaps related to grants have been calculated.

Achievable—The nonprofit has assessed its position regarding its ability to submit successful grant applications.

Relevant—The organization has adopted the mindset that grants require experience and diligence to execute particular funding area tasks successfully.

Time-bound—The grant proposal writer and team accept that the grant process must be ongoing while meeting deadlines to achieve outcomes and impacts.

Getting Grant-ready 1.0 – The Process

Being grant-ready is not easy. Being prepared by having all of the content and documents, either required or anticipated, for grant applications will make life a whole lot easier and take much of the dread out of grant proposal writing. By taking some time upfront to pull everything together, countless hours are saved every time an application deadline occurs. This will also let you know what content and documents are prepared or assembled.

Below is a mostly comprehensive list of recommended documents and information to have ready. Electronic versions of this information and content are necessary; keep hard copies as a backup. As a side note, knowing where to find these files on your laptop or PC and in a shared-file system within your organization is also indispensable. The names of these documents should also be familiar to you and the team to find them easily. Searching takes valuable time. Not every document in this list will be required for every proposal. Those with an asterisk are most commonly expected. Even if the organization does not have a tidy folder of grant-ready documents, this information is likely somewhere within the nonprofit. The following is not an exhaustive list because any funder can ask for information relevant to its funding initiatives.

- Letter of Determination from IRS*
- Organization's EIN*
- Incorporation documents from the State
- Organization background/history
- Mission Statement*
- Needs Assessment and/or Statement*
- Program/Project Description*
- Program/Project Sustainability Statement and/or Plan
- List of Key Staff
- List of Board of Directors and their Affiliations*
- Resumes/Bios of Key Staff and Board of Directors Members
- (Organizational) Budget (annual); budget narrative (annual) for organization*
- Program/Project Budget (1 year)*; budget narrative
- Program/Project Evaluation Methods*
- List of Strategic Partnerships
- List of other funding, including pending and in-kind
- Letters of Support
- Memorandums of Agreement/Memorandums of Understanding
- National Taxonomy of Exempt Entities (NTEE) Code(s)
- Code of Ethics
- Executive Summary (organization, program/project)
- Conflict of Interest Policy
- Diversity, Equity, Inclusion, and Access (CEIA) Policy
- Other policies—Nondiscrimination Policy, Technology Use Policy, Financial Management Policies
- Program participant, partner Testimonials
- Program/Project Logic Model
- Certificate of Good Standing, if State-required

I will not apologize if this list seems formidable. This is what it takes to best position the organization for funding, particularly grant funding. If you are going to apply for grants, know what is involved and understand what it takes not to waste time, energy, and money on grant applications; also, understand what is involved if the grant is awarded. It is okay if an organization decides not to pursue grant funding. That decision should be made collaboratively with the key staff and the board of directors, with constructive input from appropriate advisors. Not every nonprofit relies on grant money to be sustainable or carry out its mission.

Getting Grant-ready 2.0 – The Considerations

If an organization is new or small, it might not have focused on some business aspects that better positions it for grant awards. If a new or small nonprofit wants to play in the big leagues (which I hope you do, or I would ask, "Why did you start a nonprofit?"), you have to conduct activities similar to those in the big leagues do. And by big leagues, I do mean a five million dollar or larger budget. The best positions of the competition, as well as those concerning your sustainability, must be contemplated. With some organizations that have been established longer, complacency sets in, and certain aspects of the nonprofit business may not be reviewed or updated as frequently as they should. So, what are these considerations?

Do you know how much money is budgeted, and for what? The prospect of grant money is exciting, like finishing your first 5k. But like any good runner, you need to warm up before you can run at the front of the pack. You have to know how much is required to meet budget needs precisely and for what—program/project implementation, individual components of a program/project, operations, technology, volunteer efforts, fundraising support, or sponsorship, to name a few. A few considerations with which to get started:

- Do not expect to fund more than 30% of your total budget with grant funding.
- What portion of the other 70% is already secured (not just applied for or pledged)?
- What are the funding resources that complement the anticipated grant awards?

Here are a few more considerations.

- When considering the total planned from the grant funding portion of the overall funding strategy, do you know the gap between the budget and the amount secured from grants?
- "What gaps in the funding strategy need to be filled?"
- "What parts of the program are not funded yet?"
- "What does the funding criteria of the grant look like?"
- "Can the gaps be filled from that criteria?"

The formula for determining the funding gap is calculated by subtracting the total secured funds from the total budget:

Total Program/Project Budget - Total Secured Funds = The Gap

Here is an example:

Program Budget = $81,580

Grants strategy = (20% of budget) = $16,316 program budget from grants

Secured grant awards (not just applied for or pledged) = $6,500

$16,316 - $6,500 = $9,816 gap in grant funding

Competition lurks, and reality bites. This means that not every grant for which is applied will be awarded; industry award estimates range from 10% to 20%. There is plenty of worthy competition for every funder's dollars. And in reality grants, like sales, are a numbers game. This consideration is why ONLY the awarded (i.e., secured) grant money is used in calculating the gap.

The nonprofit's website is often where first impressions about an organization are made. Some considerations about your online presence include, but are not limited to:

- ✓ HTTPS:// (secured site)
- ✓ Does your website tell visitors that the organization has IRS tax-exempt status?
- ✓ Is the EIN on the website?
- ✓ Donation platform—do not direct online donations to a third-party page
- ✓ .org extension on URL (instead of .com, .net, .biz, etc.)
- ✓ List of key staff and Board of Directors/Trustees

- ✓ Is the website up-to-date?
- ✓ Info@myorgnamehere.org email is not enough. There should be a person to email. (By choosing to head or work for a nonprofit, you inadvertently agree to relinquish some anonymity.)
- ✓ Does the online presence feature a landing page that includes a call to action? (As of Autumn 2020, that's the trend!)

You need to understand why these considerations matter in grant award decisions. It is about clarity, transparency, accountability, and attention to detail.

Is your message (i.e., mission) clear? Your heart and soul are rooted in your mission, notably if you founded the organization. However, just because it all makes sense to you does not mean the message is clear and concise to the rest of the world. People should knowingly nod when the mission is briefly explained. If there are expressions or utterances accented with a question mark, then the message about the mission might need some rethinking. If significant confusion persists after reworking the wording, you might need to reconsider the mission itself. It has to make sense for the grant reviewer, not just you.

Is your message (i.e., mission) rooted in evidence? Do not fret if the answer is "No." or "I'm not sure." If you feel strongly about something and advocate for it, then you have a mission. Any mission can have programs/projects and impacts. However, not all missions are viewed equally by grant funders. Evidence-based missions are viewed more favorably. Evidence-based needs and their missions are best positioned for grant funding. It is best when quantitative (numerical) and qualitative (empirical) proof confirms a need exists, proving that the mission is evidence-based.

Funding often focuses on changing with the times. Be realistic. Although the mission and activities are important and improve lives in a specific community, some missions simply benefit from higher funder priorities than others. It means there is a greater focus on specific missions and activities than on others at various times. This does not mean that your mission and activities are not essential or worthy of grants and other partnerships.

Another consideration is the capacity of the organization or development department. Capacity is the amount that something can produce. The development-specific capacity considerations in a nonprofit might include: Are donors thanked within 24 hours? Does the nonprofit have the time, personnel (staff, volunteers), will/intention, plan, facilities, equipment, and supplies to successfully implement the program/project's activities? Does the organization have the number of people, places, and things to produce intended impacts?

Capacity can also relate to competence. Competency is the ability to do something successfully or efficiently. Do the people, places, and things for program/project implementation combine to operate successfully and efficiently?

Remember, a grant is a contract. It is imperative to fully understand the parameters, rules, reporting, and deadlines if the grant award is accepted. Consider if the people, places, and things successfully and efficiently complete the parameters, rules, reporting, and deadlines of the grant for which you think you want to secure?

Capacity-building (for grants): Building capacity to be best positioned for grant funding is a consideration beyond knowing the organization's capacity. Capacity-building should be purposeful. Here is something to consider: Funders want to be engaged. Companies want to know who and what they are helping improve the community. If you want volunteers or board members from a company with a community giving program (to boost your organization on their priority list or meet a grant requirement), engage with them, contact them. The worse that can happen is a "No."

There are more than 10,500 nonprofits in Central Ohio, for example. How can one company or foundation (i.e., funder) possibly learn about all of them? Consider moving your organization higher on its priority list through increased awareness about the organization through capacity-building. Build the organization's capacity to be best positioned for grant awards.

You cannot wait for "it" to knock on your door. If you want a more engaged board, find it. If you want to expand the development department, expand it. If parts of the organization are not functioning at 100%, improve or increase the capacity to be better positioned for grant awards.

Is the organization's branding consistent, concise, and conscientious? Branding is tangible (a distinctive wording or design used to identify a particular type or kind of something) and intangible (a specific identity or image regarded as an asset). Branding, in most business entities, contributes to sustainability and credibility. Branding is not a direct requirement for grant money, but sustainability and credibility are. Consistency in branding requires an action being done the same way every time, unchanging in nature, standard, or effect. It is compatibility and agreement among actions across the board, every time. Concise is verbal and nonverbal messages that are brief but comprehensive. Conscientious means to do one's work or duty well and thoroughly

Nonprofit branding encompasses so much more than a logo or color scheme on the website and letterhead. Following are some branding considerations:

- How board members are vetted, invited, and on-boarded
- How volunteers are recruited, retained, and recognized
- The hiring process, regardless of role
- Operating policies and procedures
- Fonts along with their colors and size, margins, spacing, formatting, et al. in all documents
- Consistent messaging in Program/Project Descriptions, Needs Statements, Executive Summaries, budgets and budget narratives, annual reports, 990 narratives, and marketing pieces
- Distinct messages in mission, vision, and purpose statements
- Up-to-date and accurate information across all channels

I get these things require time and, in some cases, money. Sorry to be blunt, but you should have known that when you incorporated as a nonprofit, as a nonprofit BUSINESS. It is helpful to apply for-profit, traditional business practices to nonprofits. Understanding the elements that for-profit businesses consider makes sense as we remember that 501(c)3 is a tax status, not a business model. For-profit companies understand the strengths, weaknesses, opportunities, and threats to their business. This analysis is referred to as a SWOT analysis (S=strengths, W=weaknesses, O=opportunities, and T=threats). Nonprofits should have the same awareness. Nonprofits can determine their grant readiness by analyzing the strengths, weaknesses, opportunities, and threats concerning grant funding.

Depending upon the stage or condition of Getting Grant-ready 2.0—The Considerations within an organization, each strength or weakness or opportunity or threat relating to grant funding affects best-positioning. The positioning can be formally assessed through a SWOT analysis. A SWOT analysis is an assessment tool generally presented in a four-quadrant chart to evaluate your strengths, weaknesses, opportunities, and threats. Definitions seem elementary, but establishing common ground is integral to being on common ground when learning SWOT analyses. A solid grant strategy cannot be built without a solid foundation. Therefore, here are the definitions of the elements of a SWOT analysis. Strength is the capacity to withstand great force or pressure. A weakness is a quality or feature regarded as a disadvantage or fault. Opportunity is a circumstance or set of circumstances making it possible to progress or grow. A threat is the possibility of trouble, danger, or ruin.

Let's build on that base. For grant funding purposes, strengths are the factors and characteristics that may be considered favorable for the organization or program/project; weaknesses are the factors and characteristics deemed detrimental. Opportunities are the factors and characteristics that are advantageous to the organization or program/project; threats are the factors and characteristics that pose potential failure. The SWOT analysis facilitates identifying and categorizing the afore-mentioned grant-ready considerations.

There are internal and external factors and characteristics that help determine each of the four SWOT elements. Internal factors and characteristics impact strengths and weaknesses. They reflect the current condition. External factors influence opportunities and threats. They anticipate possible detractors. Internal factors include but are not limited to:

- human resources (staff, volunteers, board members)
- target constituency
- physical resources (location, building, equipment, technology)
- financial assets (grants and other funding streams, additional revenue)
- activities and processes (programs/projects, systems and implementation)
- sustainability (experiences, reputation, partnerships)

- organizational structure

External factors include but are not limited to:
- political issues
- environmental issues
- availability of strategic alliances
- governmental or policy restrictions or legislation
- demographics and social determinants (age, race, gender, culture of those in the community to be served)
- the economy
- events (local, national, global)
- future trends

External factors can affect internal ones with more significant consequences than the reverse scenario. For example, threats might not have developed into weaknesses yet, but they should be monitored to avoid becoming a danger to sustainability. Additionally, any opportunity can be nurtured into a strength; the reverse is not possible.

In the for-profit world, outlining a company's strengths allows managers to isolate factors and characteristics that might suggest logical actions, such as expansion, or which strengths could be used to counteract weaknesses; likewise, with weaknesses. We can make the same assimilation for grant funding (and in all nonprofit operations' areas, for that matter). A logical conclusion can be made about best-positioning for grant funding or how to move an opportunity to a strength by having a concise snapshot of how the organization or program/project is positioned. In the same way, if a particular weakness that is potentially a "red flag" for a grant funder is identified, that factor can be mitigated, corrected, or perhaps make the decision not to apply for that particular grant. Here is what I mean:

The ABC Foundation has enjoyed 501(c)3 status for 17 years, has been sustainable, and experienced some growth operating the same way all 17 years. They have no paid operations staff and seemingly operate with only a Board of Directors. The Founder is the President of the Board. Typically, there would be the governance team (the board) and the Executive team (the staff) for operations in a nonprofit entity. Having no Executive team is a "red flag" to many funders. This arrangement might lead to questions of transparency, for example. Lack of transparency is a weakness. A big weakness. ABC Foundation might choose to be more traditionally structured by adding a paid or unpaid Executive staff to be better positioned for grant funding. They can also decide if they need grant funding—if grant funding is necessary to support what has been successful for 17 years. (If it isn't broken, don't fix it!)

Additionally, a SWOT analysis can reveal how strongly positioned the organization or program/project is for grant funding, perhaps indicating a higher ask is possible. The stronger the positioning, the higher the ask's dollar amount can be because better positioning reflects transparency, capacity, and sustainability. One indication of strong positioning is if there are more strengths and opportunities than weaknesses and threats in the analysis. Another is incorporating a weakness or threat into the Needs Statement. A weakness or threat might also be integrated with outputs and intended impacts of the program/project description. (Needs Statement, outputs and impacts, and Program/Project and Evaluation Methods descriptions are particularized in subsequent blocks.)

SWOT analysis can be a strategic tool. Remember, the reason for completing a SWOT analysis is to gain helpful perspectives, such as uncovering positive forces for collaboration and recognizing potential problems necessitating being addressed. Be strategic with what the SWOT reveals. Use strengths to take advantage of opportunities, such as grant funding. By taking advantage of opportunities, weaknesses can be overcome. For example, if the numbers (quantity) receiving services are less than desired or budgeted, it is a weakness. That weakness can be overcome (i.e., numbers increased) by taking advantage of grant funding to expand the efforts. Another strategy for best-positioning is to use strengths to avoid threats. Identifying opportunities can also thwart threats. Suggestions for using a SWOT analysis to best position the organization or program/project for grants include:

- Identify issues or problems needing change or improvement
- Set/reaffirm purposes and targets
- Create actionable item(s), strategic plans(s)
- Explore options for solutions to problems

- Adjust and refine plans mid-course, identifying new opportunities and threats
- Identify opportunities for success in the context of threats to success to clarify directions and choices
- Determine where change is possible; an inventory of strengths and weaknesses can disclose priorities and possibilities

Just as the strengths and weaknesses of an organization are identified from an internal perspective, do not ignore people's views outside your group. Cogitate strengths and weaknesses from all stakeholder perspectives, including those receiving services. Do others see problems (or assets) that you do not? What is reported from all perspectives? A SWOT analysis is not a resume; it is a report card. Analyze and develop insights about your organization's exact condition. As you execute the SWOT analysis, it is deficient if asking only, "What is our organization's biggest weakness?" You have to go to the next step and scrutinize how the weakness developed or why this area was neglected. It also helps to consider your strengths as areas to improve even more. For example, high engagement on social media can be leveraged for a higher percentage of those supporters to donate. Following is a sample SWOT Analysis conducted for the Mentoring Individuals with Disabilities Flip It Reverse Job and Career Fair.

SWOT Analysis—MIWD
Flip It Reverse Job and Career Fair

STRENGTHS	WEAKNESSES
- No competition - Disability inclusion is a broader initiative than ever before - Comprehensive program components - Developed with vocational rehabilitation professionals - Job seekers with disabilities participating in VR job development programs or not can participate - Robust volunteer engagement in the community - Business community indicates	- Nonprofit is a young organization - Lack of familiarity with reverse job and career fair model - Trends in VR job development models - Competitive environment for cause-driven funding and sponsorships - Myths about hiring people with disabilities

the need and desire for DI information and engagement	
OPPORTUNITIES • No competition • Traditional full- and part-time job opportunities • Increased awareness of the return on investment of employees with disabilities • Securing community and funding partners	THREATS • Flip It Reverse Job and Career Fair is a new opportunity in the area • Economy • Competitive environment for cause-driven funding and sponsorships • Lack of familiarity with reverse job and career fair model

Now that you know what it takes to be grant-ready, could you recognize when NOT to submit the grant application? It is not as easy to learn this process as it is to know your organization is getting grant-ready. The allure of money can be powerful and misleading. When you are confident in readiness, you can discern when to delay or walk away from a grant opporunity. By fully understanding the staffing levels, staff's expertise, restrictions of facilities, funding gap(s), competition, and more, you can quickly determine if the capacity exists to be able to fulfill the (contractual) obligations of the grant agreement if awarded. Almost is never enough.

Being grant-ready is a mindset. It is natural to want to jump in and start writing that grant proposal. However, it is pragmatic to know what applying for grants means for the nonprofit beyond its monetary value.

Finding and Vetting Grant Opportunities

I think it is time to find those grant opportunities now. You have a firm understanding of what grant funding is and what it will mean for the organization. Begrudgingly, you understand the mindset and process of being grant-ready. The gaps in the funding strategy have been identified—the parts of the program or project compel more money to meet the budget, or perhaps other parts of the organization's budget such as capital projects, technology upgrades, volunteer recognition, or even general operating expenses. It is clear what should be considered before applying for grant money.

It might sound counterintuitive, but we are going to figure out how to track the grant opportunities and information before figuring out where to find them and how to vet them. Most fundraising and donor management platforms include grant tracking modules. While convenient and report-generating, these modules are not as comprehensive as most development strategies require. Most grant funding strategies use other tools in place of or to complement fundraising software.

The first step is selecting the best tool for the organization for tracking. Choose a tool that is flexible, customizable, and user-friendly. Create a framework to track grant opportunities. Preparation and organization circumvent a shot-gun approach to writing proposals. It is difficult to find something better than an Excel spreadsheet. The spreadsheet created by **SMART Money Grant Writing** is an excellent place to start. Our template is named Grants Tracker and can be downloaded from the **SMART Money Grant Writing** website for free. Column headers include the funder name, the funding gap addressed (program/project, general operating, technology, volunteer, staff and professional development, and more funding needs), the funder's location, the funder's focus or area(s) of interest, whether the funds are restricted or unrestricted, a link to the funder's information or submission portal, deadline for submission or dates of their grant cycle, the nonprofit's internally assigned submission deadline, method/process of submission, ask amount, award amount or decline decision, previous award (if any), the date the application was submitted, anticipated notification of award/decline date, mid-year report due date (if an awarded grant has one), end-of-funding-period report due date (if any), and user name and password for that funder's site. One additional column can be added to prioritize the grant opportunities for at-a-glance review; this information should fill Column A for at-a-glance prioritizing.

On the Grants Tracker, column widths can easily be adjusted independently of each other to format as needed or desired. Using an Excel spreadsheet (or similar spreadsheet) allows for sorting and prioritizing by any criteria required at a given moment. Even with all of this information, the spreadsheet can be printed with all of the information on one page by using landscape orientation and scaling to fit all columns on one page. The print will be small, but viewing so much material without flipping through multiple pages is beneficial when planning and strategizing. For reports for meetings or email attachments, save the Excel workbook as a PDF.

The Grants Tracker includes much information about the funder, including the name, location, focus or mission, funding restrictions, website link, submission deadline or grant cycle information, method/process to apply, and anticipated notification or award date. The funder location can be helpful for relationship building or prioritization purposes. The Grants Tracker includes grants management information for the organization's internal use, such as the funding need or gap, assigned deadline, any previous awards, date of proposal submission, the ask amount, and the username and password for the submission portal. The labels of the columns and content to fill in on the Grants Tracker include:

- Funder—name of grantmaker
- Funding Need—organization's funding need
- Funder's Location—city, state where grantmaker is located
- Funder's Focus, Mission—initiatives supported by grantmaker
- Restricted, Unrestricted—funds are restricted to specific spending, have no spending restrictions
- Link to application info, submission portal—link to grantmaker website and/or submission portal

- Funder Deadline/Grant Cycle—grantmaker's deadline or grant cycle deadline(s)
- Assigned Submission Deadline—organization's internally assigned deadline to submit
- Method (LOI, online, etc.)—grantmaker's process or system to apply
- Ask Amount—amount requested in the ask/proposal
- Awarded or Declined—indicate awarded and the amount or declined to fund
- Previous Award—any awards from grantmaker of earlier applications
- Date Proposal Submitted—date the organization submitted the proposal
- Anticipated Award Date—date grantmaker is expected to announce awards/decline
- Mid-Year Report Due Date—date the interim report(s) are due (if any)
- Year-End Report Due Date—date the final report is due at the end of the funding period
- User Name—organization's user name for grantmaker's portal
- Password—organization's password for grantmaker's portal

The primary reason for the Funder Deadline/Grant Cycle and Assigned Deadline columns is for prioritizing. Some grant applications have designated deadlines, and some have ongoing (non-designated) ones. The Funder Deadline/Grant Cycle column is for the exact deadline date identified through the funder's guidelines. If there is no deadline date, but instead, the cycle is ongoing, that should be noted in the Deadline Info column in place of a hard date. With ongoing, non-date-specific deadlines, a firm date can be selected and entered into the Assigned Deadline column. Every grant application to be submitted should have an assigned deadline. As funding opportunities are vetted, the Assigned Deadline column should have firm dates by which proposal submissions are planned internally. By assigning a date rather than leaving that cell empty or identifying it as "ongoing," human nature takes over to raise its importance, creating a sense of urgency and keeping it on your radar.

A column for notes can be added to any Grants Tracker. It is a good idea to abbreviate notes and use them as reminders. The funder's link is handy for referring to details and other lengthier content about the grant opportunity rather than having lengthy comments and notes on the spreadsheet.

Although tempting, creating a list of grantmakers in name alone is a waste of time. In the same thought process, as an organization must spend money (on a grant proposal writer) to obtain grant money, the time spent finding and vetting grants is some of the most valuable time and effort spent in development or fundraising. However, a list of grantmakers' names is a good start, and that is the first column to fill in on the Grants Tracker; but where are those names found? Now is when we set the Grants Tracker aside and find the grant opportunities to fill it. It is important to remember that this list is of potential funders. Not every name associated with the funding opportunities will be a viable opportunity.

Ok, you know how much is required and for what. Where are grantmakers found that have the criteria that fit? Grant opportunities are not as difficult to find as one thinks. Here are some resources.

Perform an internet search for the funding topic, mission, or program/project. Adapt these examples:

grant funding for job development for people with disabilities

grant funding for job development grants for workforce development grant

funding for volunteer initiatives

grants for volunteer initiatives in State/City, State

Narrowing the parameters can help reduce overwhelming results.

Search individual corporate and corporate foundation websites. Not all corporations have foundations, but many have community-giving programs without formal foundations. A variety of businesses distribute their philanthropy dollars from their marketing departments. Learn to identify community-giving sections on company websites.

Explore grant funding and funder databases*.

- Foundation Directory Online (FDO) is found at Candid.org. FDO maintains the most comprehensive databases of grantmakers. It is fee-based, and it is not cheap. However, it can be accessed at no charge in many locations throughout most states. Most major library systems have access through at least one license, usually hosted at their primary location (not via remote online access). The databases include grantmakers for nonprofit, for-profit, small businesses, and individual grants. If you do not have access in your community, perhaps a community foundation or other nonprofit support or advocates group in your area does and allows access through their membership.

In mid-2020, FDO made part of their database available online at no charge; the user is required to create a free account. However, many of the filter features that are crucial to targeted grant searches are not available online. These filters are what set FDO apart from all other grant database services.

- Foundation Directory Online Maps is also found at Candid.org. This feature can create compelling snapshots to help make the case. Based on search parameters, it shows exactly where the funding is going. While that picture can be discouraging, it can make a great case to grantmakers for the program/project, especially if not in urban areas or areas that are more heavily funded, because the necessity for funding can be visually demonstrated based on the map. Perhaps this is an unintended use of the feature, but it can support an urgent call to action.
- GrantStation is found at GrantStation.com and is a membership-based database of many grant opportunities in the U.S.
- GrantWatch, found at GrantWatch.com, is another fee-based grant service with many grant listings.

(*Database resource listings are intended as information and not an endorsement of any resources.)

Government agency grant websites and web pages have opportunities that are updated frequently. Most offer newsletters or other notification registrations to know when new opportunities become available.

- **Community foundations'** statewide associations or groups are established in most states. OANO (Ohio Association of Nonprofit Organizations) and the Florida Nonprofit Alliance are a couple of examples. Some nonprofit service areas have more than one community foundation from which to have support. Getting registered with all supporting the service area is the first step to building a relationship with them.
- **Philanthropy news publications and websites** are other resources that regularly post grant opportunities. There are multiple philanthropy news publications. Examples include Philanthropy News Digest, Nonprofit Quarterly, and The Chronicle of Philanthropy.
- **Organizational newsletters** from the business giving partners, corporate foundations, and nonprofit and professional consulting firms offer digital communications subscriptions. (I once signed up for an out-of-state accounting firm's grants list and received a list of more than 300 viable funders, most of which I had never found in traditional databases.)
- **Networking, listening, and common sense!** Pay attention. Look around. For example, the local library will have a placard of their board members. Take note of the companies with which each is associated. Check for community giving of local and regional companies. Separately, one-location businesses can have deep pockets and robust philanthropy. Social media can reveal obscure funding resources and divulge thought-provoking tidbits about some grantmakers.

This is not an exhaustive list because the networking, listening, and common sense resources are nearly limitless. At a minimum, block a few hours every month on the calendar to look in on potential funders for new postings and information by browsing brochures, websites, media, social media, annual reports, newsletters, and blogs.

The next step is to determine which of those names are viable funding opportunities for your organization and its budgetary gaps. This is the vetting process. Investigating. Researching. While finding grants seems easy enough, vetting grant opportunities is much more complex and time-consuming than one thinks. It is vital to find the funding that fits. It is vital to vet the specifics:

- What are the funding guidelines put forth by the funder? Is there an alignment between those guidelines (criteria) and your organization's mission or projects/programs?

- What is the deadline to apply? Are there ongoing or date-specific deadlines? Are there multiple grant cycles throughout the year for the same funding focus? Are there numerous grant cycles with varying deadlines based on the funder's focus or area of interest?

- Type of funding—project-specific, mission-specific, restricted/unrestricted, operating, capital, matching funds requirements, or other types

- Process—Letter of Intent/Letter of Inquiry (LOI), Request for Proposal (RFP), not accepting unsolicited proposals, online application only, free form or fill-in online application, Or mail or fax processes.

- Is a Letter of Intent or Letter of Inquiry (LOI) required? An LOI summarizes a full proposal for which funders might ask, streamlining their process. From the LOIs, the funder will invite a limited number of full proposals to be submitted. A newer trend similar to an LOI is a summary email requested by the grantmaker in advance of submitting or being invited to submit a full proposal. The funder will indicate whether the LOI should follow or be completed on a specific form or be presented in a freeform style. The title Letter of Introduction is interchangeable with Intent or Inquiry.

- Will an RFP be released? RFP stands for Request for Proposal. Most corporate and community grants do not use an RFP process. Government offices and agencies primarily use this more formal process.

- Are they accepting unsolicited proposals? Assume the grantmaker accepts applications according to their deadlines if there is no phrase similar to "Not accepting unsolicited applications." "Not accepting unsolicited proposals" is a polite way for the funder to proclaim they have already decided who or what

they are funding!
- How will the information be submitted or transmitted? The most common is an online application. What is the style of the online application—freeform or fill-in online application? Does the proposal need to be submitted through email, traditional mail, or fax?
- Organizational structure: Is tax-exempt status required? Can the program/project be fiscally sponsored by a Fiduciary Agent?

Check GuideStar.org or Candid.org to find the grantmaker's mission and check the most recent 990 for focuses and organizations they funded and for what amount. The IRS Charitable Division also posts 990s.

In addition to thoroughly reading through the guidelines, there are additional ways to learn if the opportunity and/or grantmaker is a good fit. A funder's IRS Form 990 has much valuable information. Besides contact names and addresses (found on the first page of the form), the information in Parts I.1., III.1., and VII. Sections A and B disclose their focus, mission, advocacies, board members, and key staff. More interestingly, other organizations or programs/projects the grantmaker has supported are listed in Schedule A, Part II. The best resource to locate a funder's Form 990 is Guidestar.org or Candid.org. Form 990s can also be found on the IRS website in the charitable organization section. Annual reports are also a valuable source funder research and are often posted online.

Create a funding matrix system—Excel spreadsheet (i.e., Grants Tracker), notebook, index cards, sticky notes on the office wall, or whiteboard. Grant tracking modules in donor management software are also a helpful tracking resource.

SMART grant opportunity vetting follows these guidelines:

Specific—The organization has identified all gaps in grant funding. The organization has identified all of the information about its programs/projects and all operations required by grantmakers.

Measurable—Funding gaps related to grants have been calculated. The identified grant opportunities will partially or entirely fill the gaps.

Achievable—The funders' guidelines closely align with the gaps and timing of the nonprofit.

Relevant—The funder's focus or area of interest closely aligns with the program/project or other funding gaps.

Time-bound—The submission deadline is within the organization's capacity to meet, and the expected award date allows ample time to use the funds for the intended and promised purpose.

Once a viable grant opportunity is discovered from any search category, track it.

Regardless of the category searched for grant opportunities, how is it determined to be a good fit? Determining the fit is well worth spending, on average, up to 30 minutes on one funder to examine the funder's criteria or guidelines. Skimming causes headaches later. If details are skimmed over, a geographic restriction or other nuance might be missed, later eliminating that grant from the list. Only valid grants go on the Grants Tracker. When vetting potential grants, fill in as many cells on the spreadsheet as possible. If not enough cells or not the right ones are checked or filled, scrap that grant, and move on. Time is too valuable to be wasted on an application that does not fit. Spending ten more minutes researching that grantmaker saves copious time and energy later.

Some grantmakers offer more than one submission cycle during a calendar year. In some cases, to facilitate multiple awards throughout the year, usually allowing one award per organization per year. In other cases, it is grants management on the funder's part. A grantmaker might have several focuses and set different submission deadlines for each area of interest to better manage to review the applications. If there are multiple cycles, track all pertinent deadlines individually on the Grants Tracker.

The last step in completing the Grants Tracker is prioritizing. Prioritization is not a one-and-done activity. Just as programs/projects should be evaluated periodically or at designated intervals to recalibrate if necessary, so does the grant process. Depending upon the funding strategy and targets met, the grants strategy can be sorted and prioritized by any column on the Grants Tracker. Updates requested by the Board might require a different prioritization than reevaluating funding gaps. The budget might change during a fiscal year, making yet another set of grant data necessary. New grant opportunities can be added and prioritized as well.

Advanced grants tracking: A version of the Grants Tracker assigns a value to the vetting process's primary considerations for optimal prioritization. One additional column can be added to prioritize the grant opportunities for at-a-glance review. As mentioned earlier, this at-a-glance information should fill Column A. Here is how to prioritize by values (importance): Columns for Funder Focus, Funder Deadline/Grant Cycle, Funder Award Amount, and Anticipated Award Date are given values between 1 and 5 (5 being most valuable, meets most or all criteria). The values of that vetted information are added together, resulting in a value system for prioritization. Hypothetically, opportunities scoring 16 or higher would be considered "must apply" grants. Those scoring between 10 and 15 would be scheduled in the second tier of importance. Those scoring below an agreed-upon total (9 in our hypothetical prioritization) would be removed altogether. The organization or grants team sets the score point levels for action. Values can change as funding gaps are broadened, reduced, or eliminated. Additionally, Restricted and Unrestricted can be included in the vetting value, depending upon the strategy or urgency. A zero value is given for restricted and a value of 5 for unrestricted funds (values 1 through 4 are not used). Color coding is another option for defining priorities.

One final comment on prioritizing possible grants: Be realistic with hometown philanthropy. Unfortunately, there are "politics" in the nonprofit world, particularly when money is involved. The larger the funding and funder, the bigger the proverbial "bang for their buck" is expected. This is why evidence-based programs/projects, substantial fiduciary transparency, useable data and metrics, strong leadership, relatable storytelling, and a diverse and active Board of Directors are essential to grant proposal writing. These contribute to relationship and reputation building for the organization. Funders fund people, not programs/projects; they fund the people served by the program/project. However, they also fund the people implementing the program/project. If yours is the smaller or newer program for job development for people with disabilities, be realistic that it is not the $15-million-budgeted local nonprofit that is part of a nationally known name established 80 years ago. Be realistic that larger dollar amounts go to larger budgets and better-known organizations because their intended impact is more significant, ROI is higher, exposure of partnerships has more benefits, and related "politics" are in play. If the program budget is $17,000 annually, be realistic about the grant funding from larger grantmakers; consider sponsorships, volunteer opportunities, and board positions to build the relationship for eventual grant funding.

With a firm understanding and commitment to finding and vetting grant opportunities, you should be able to create a strategic and qualified grants plan and recognize when to eliminate a possible grant from the list. The allure of money can be powerful and misleading but can be worth the effort and time.

Tarra Nystrom

Let's Write the Grant Proposal

Cover Sheets and Cover Letters for Grant Proposals

A Cover Sheet or Cover Letter can be of great value beyond perfunctory information. Both documents identify the information attached therein, provide basic information about the grant request, and either is the first page of the packet unless otherwise directed, but the similarities end there. Not all grant applications require a Cover Sheet or Cover Letter, but including one is expected. Understanding the differences between the two documents can help comply with grant submission requirements and avoid the submission ending up in the reject pile.

A grant Cover Sheet is a form for entering specific information required by the funding organization. The form limits the amount of information provided to answer the questions. Usually, grant funders requiring a Cover Sheet provide the form. The information requested includes the name and contact information of the organization, the Employer Identification Number (EIN), and the purpose and amount of the ask. It usually includes information the foundation uses to screen applications. Some Cover Sheet forms include spaces for brief program/project description, organization history, or the population served.

A grant Cover Letter is often the first opportunity to introduce the nonprofit's mission and demonstrate alignment with the funder's focus. Unlike the Cover Sheet, the Cover Letter is a formal letter addressed to the grantmaker and signed by the nonprofit's Executive Director. The Cover Letter is no more than one page, preferably on letterhead stationery. The Cover Letter is not an Executive Summary.

There is an advisable format for a Cover Letter. A grant proposal Cover Letter begins with an introductory paragraph that includes a brief statement about the grant request's purpose and amount. Remember, *purpose* refers to the use of the money, not the purpose of the organization. The letter continues by providing a brief history of the organization, describing the program/project and how it relates to the organization's mission, and discussing the program/project's expected outcome in no more than two paragraphs. This information can be condensed and connected by using transitional words. For example: "Since our founding in 2011, Mentoring Individuals with Disabilities has focused on disability inclusion in the workplace." This sentence provides some history and a reference to the mission and program focus. (It also uses a transition word; its usefulness is explained in the block on "Storytelling for Grant Proposals.") The final paragraph includes contact information.

A few pointers for Cover Letters:

- Be succinct.
- Get to the point quickly.
- Do not repeat proposal content verbatim.
- Use Cover Letters for corporate and private foundation funding asks; do not use them with government grant proposals.
- Follow proper business letter formatting regarding date, inside address, and salutation.
- Do not use a salutation of "To Whom It May Concern." Confirm the funder's contact person and correct spelling of their name.
- Use the same date on the Cover Letter as the completed grant application.
- Convey a strong understanding of the funder and how the grant proposal aligns with the funder's focus
- Include one evidence-based point that demonstrates a need for this program/project.
- Write after the rest of the proposal has been written.
- Use the final paragraph to emphasize what the funding partnership will mean for the target group being served.
- Depending upon the proximity to the grantmaker, consider including an invitation to visit your organization.
- Close with "Sincerely."

- Include "ENCLOSURE" at the bottom of the letter, even if it will be sent digitally.
- Avoid sounding cute or clever.
- Avoid sounding like too much of an expert.
- Use advanced editing software to polish grammar, spelling, and punctuation.
- Do not use storytelling content (i.e., a story about a client or other stakeholder).
- Use standard 1" margins on organizational letterhead.
- If the letter exceeds one page, edit the content—do not decrease the font or the margins.
- If you replicate the template at the end of this block, the Cover Letter will be formatted correctly.

If a Cover Sheet or Cover Letter is not part of the application form, there is an option to use a free-form Sheet or Letter as an attachment. The extra effort of a well-written Cover Letter sets you above the competition.

SMART Cover Letters and Cover Sheets following these guidelines:

Specific—The content is explicit to the grant opportunity. The content and formatting follow grantmaker guidelines if any.

Measurable—The content summarizes the organization's capacity and program/project and may generally address qualitative and quantitative aspects of the program/project related to the ask.

Achievable—The content only addresses the information within the grant proposal to ensure only the outputs, outcomes, and impacts tied to the grant are covered.

Relevant—The content only addresses the information within the grant proposal, which is closely connected to the funder's focus.

Time-bound—The Cover Sheet or Letter is grant proposal-specific.

Sample Cover Sheet 1:

Mentoring Individuals with Disabilities
[Organization Logo]

Flip It Reverse Job & Career Fair Funding Proposal
April 2020

Tarra Nystrom, MBA
Director of Development
1234 Your Street, City, State Zip
www.MIWD.org
Tarra@miwd.org 614/555-8246

Sample Cover Sheet 2:

Mentoring Individuals with Disabilities

[Organization Logo]

Flip It Reverse Job & Career Fair Funding Proposal

April 2020

Flip It Reverser Job and Career Fair for individuals with disabilities and companies with a need for talented, qualified employees.

The vision of the program is to connect job seekers with disabilities with business owners and hiring managers by turning the tables on traditional job fairs. These connections will create job and career opportunities with sustainable, living wages for employees with disabilities while filling critical roles within companies with qualified individuals from an underutilized talent pool.

We are seeking a partnership of $5,000.00 with the Weisenberger Family Foundation.

Tarra Nystrom, MBA
Director of Development
1234 Your Street, City, State Zip
www.MIWD.org
Tarra@miwd.org 614/555-8246

Sample Cover Letter, on organizational letterhead:

July 17, 2018

Mary Smith, Ph.D.
Our Community Foundation
4321 Commerce Lane
Some City, YZ 00662

Dear Dr. Smith,

The Some City Senior Center respectfully requests a grant of $50,000 for our Senior Latino Community Outreach Pilot Project.

As the largest senior center in Any County, serving over 450 seniors daily, we are aware of the changing demographics in our service area. And we are committed to growing and adapting our center to meet the changing needs. The Senior Latino Community Outreach Pilot Project allows us to pilot a one-year effort to determine if our center can effectively:

- Provide comprehensive access to health and social services to seniors in the Latino communities served by our center
- Raise and fully integrate the cultural competency of the board, staff, and volunteers of the Some City Senior Center

Our board of directors is enthusiastic about this program. It is eager to launch it to become the most inclusive and culturally competent for seniors in all of our communities needing these essential services. Should we find at the end of our pilot year that the program is successful, our board has committed to including a portion of the program's yearly expenses into our annual budget so that the program becomes an integral part of our services.

Our Center will become the primary referral by Health Access Latino, Families of Any County, and three community clinics within 15 miles of our center through this program. We will also accept additional referrals of Spanish-speaking seniors from any other community agency in our immediate service area.

Thank you for your consideration. Please let me know if you have any questions. We also welcome the opportunity to meet with you to discuss the merits of the Some City Senior Center and the pilot program. In the meantime, Connie Smith, Director of Development, be reached at 614-555-8246 or ConnieS@SomeCtySrCtr.org.

Sincerely,

Jane Lovely Executive Director

ENCLOSURE

Organizational Information for Grant Proposals

Because no two grant applications are the same, the organization's information will most likely differ from proposal to proposal. In general, this section provides the opportunity to explain what the organization is about and prove it is competent for doing what the proposal states will be done. Shun modesty, but be able to back up about which you brag. If you complete this section free-form, exploit the information that establishes credibility and shows the capacity to implement the program/project effectively in no more than three (3) pages.

- ✓ The full legal name of the organization, including its legal status—Example: 501(c)3, including doing business as name (d/b/a/)
- ✓ The physical address of the primary location and all other sites; list a mailing address, such as a PO Box, if different from the primary location.
- ✓ Mission Statement
- ✓ Vision Statement (if the organization has one)
- ✓ Date founded
- ✓ Founding members or group(s) and the purpose the organization serves within the community, identifying the community
- ✓ Historical recap
- ✓ Bulleted list of programs and projects without descriptions
- ✓ Role in the community, including service collaborations and other partnerships
- ✓ Demographic(s) of the target group receiving services
- ✓ Niche filled by the organization, programs/projects—what makes the organization different from others in the community
- ✓ Bulleted list of successes related to the grant application, including awards,

media coverage, and other recognition
- ✓ Abridged Needs Statement
- ✓ Narrative statement of financial position, including an organizational budget, annual fundraising revenue, and relevant additional funding resources
- ✓ Synopsis of Board of Directors, key Staff, and (relevant) volunteers; if requested, bios of the same should be limited to three or four sentences emphasizing value and skills, not the personal purpose of service or beliefs
- ✓ Explain the organization's operating structure

The format of this application component might be dictated by the grantmaker through a form, perhaps with word or character restrictions. Whenever possible, take advantage of being able to create your own form by submitting comprehensive, seamless content in narrative form rather than a list. You do not have to be a prolific or confident writer to elucidate an attention-grabbing document that makes a remarkable first impression. Consider these phrases to be SMART in showing credibility and proving capacity by using them as transitions and descriptors for activities, policies and procedures, historical timelines, budgets, and financials:

Specific—"understands the need in the community"

Measurable—"financial stability"

Achievable—"delivers vital services in the community"

Relevant—"held in high regard in the community" or "diverse Board of Directors" or "staff mirroring the community"

Time-bound—"corroborates prudent management"

The organizational information will not win any awards for creativity, but it can create a remarkable first impression. The grant reviewer will be compelled to read the proposal with confidence in your organization through concise and thoughtful phrasing as well as clean formatting.

Mission Statements for Grant Proposals

Mission statements are important. This block is not intended to teach you how to craft a definitive mission statement for your nonprofit. We need to focus on how the mission statement is used in grant applications and how the origins of the mission statement influence content written for grant proposals. In that vein, we will look at the basics of mission statements, though, as we explain how to use them.

Simply, the mission statement states the purpose of the nonprofit organization. Your mission statement is an original, cohesive statement explaining what you do and why you exist. Mission statements must be clear, concise, and memorable, not cluttered with elaboration, jargon, and assorted adjectives and adverbs. A mission statement should be reviewed periodically to ensure that it reflects the organization's current purpose and trajectory because issues change; your organization and mission statement require a periodic change to remain relevant.

Because the mission statement is the foundation for all of the activities of a nonprofit, its message is an integral part of the grant proposal process. Internally, the mission statement is used to enthuse and unify staff, volunteers, and board members, including the grant proposal writing team. As programs develop and evaluation methods are designed from the mission, the outcomes and impacts closely tied to the mission can be accurately identified and anticipated. For the external stakeholder groups, the mission statement encourages and generates support by communicating impacts and aspirations to potential grantmakers, for example.

The strength of the mission statement attracts support. However, it should be used only once in a grant application. The message of the mission statement is likely to show up more than once in the content created from a grant application. The mission statement (rooted in values, norms, and beliefs) influences most other areas of your organization, guiding momentum, focusing energy and attention, igniting new ideas, shaping culture, instituting consistency, driving action, and establishing the organization's brand and message. SMART mission statements demonstrate knowledge of the concerns in the context of the community:

Specific—The mission statement is an original, cohesive statement explaining what you do and why you exist. The mission statement must be clear, concise, and memorable.

Measurable—The mission statement is used only once in a grant application. The message of the mission statement is likely to show up more than once in a grant proposal.

Achievable—Internally, the mission statement is used to enthuse and unify all internal stakeholders. For the external stakeholder groups, the mission statement encourages and generates support by communicating aims and aspirations.

Relevant—The mission statement should be reviewed periodically to ensure that it reflects the organization's current purpose and trajectory for the organization or program/project to remain significant.

Time-bound—The mission statement should be reviewed periodically to reflect the organization's current purpose and trajectory.

Occasionally, a grant application might afford the opportunity or require mission and vision statements. It is essential to understand the difference between the two. The mission statement is the "why" an organization exists, and the vision statement tells what the future looks like to achieve the mission. It is worth noting that for-profit businesses and individuals applying for grant funding should also have mission and vision statements.

- ✓ The mission statement is short and concise, explaining the organization's purpose, stated in terms of invariability and durability. It describes and summarizes the organization's activities to maintain focus.
- ✓ The vision statement is more than a statement. It describes the intended result, stated in terms of ambition, optimism, and rationale. It is beneficial for guiding the organization into the future.

The message of the mission is communicated throughout a grant proposal. The mission statement itself is shared only once. Try adding the mission statement after the proposal is completed for its most effective placement. Choose where and when strategically.

Needs Statements for Grant Proposals

Without need, there is no mission. Nonprofit work is rooted in need in a community. A need is a circumstance in which something is necessary or requires a course of action; necessity. In a community, a need stems from a living thing being diminished or damaged. In the nonprofit world, a living thing that has been diminished or damaged requires assistance from external influence (i.e., a program or project) to regain, retain, or replenish what was lost or never available.

A need, like a mission, can be anything about which passion or compassion is felt. However, a need that is viable for nonprofit program/project implementation is most viable if evidence-based. In a grant proposal, this evidence of need is expressed by a Needs Statement with the course of action required so that the program/project can be a reality. The Needs Statement defines the fundamental issue or problem. It is used to educate about the community needs that the program/project seeks to improve urgently. The purpose of the Needs Statement is to present facts and stories supporting the program/project or other funding gaps. All grant applications should include a Needs Statement.

Before composing the Needs Statement, there must be an understanding of the problem and its nature, reasons, and causes so that it is circumscriptive of importance to the organization and interest to the grantmaker. Studying statistical and anecdotal evidence of the issue, scaling the problem from national to local, and considering all perspectives, including those of the targeted population for services, lay the groundwork for the Needs Statement. Understanding the need anchors the human need with hard facts. Because the Needs Statement establishes the rationale for a program/project, it should also demonstrate comprehension of the surrounding conditions in the community, aggravating or heightening the problem. The judicious use of statistical information makes an ethical and authentic case for support.

The Needs Statement is sometimes referred to as the Problem Statement or Case for

Support. However, the Needs Statement is not the same as the Needs Assessment. The Needs Assessment is a deeper dive into the problem and need and their causes. The Needs Statement is composed of the information discovered during the Assessment. A quality Needs Assessment cites the most relevant data and comparative statistics and utilizes testimonials for the specific target population receiving services. Often the Needs Statement and Assessment include what is lacking in the community that influences or exacerbates the problem.

We know that grant applications change from opportunity to opportunity. Still, the need stays the same as long as the mission or program/project addressing the mission remains the same. With that said, the Needs Statement should be written for each funder's focus and specific to the grant ask every time. Remember, the Needs Statement is always written from the Needs Assessment (which never changes). A nonprofit can have more than one program/project or other funding gaps. Still, it must focus on the specific gap in the funding for which that grant is being applied while avoiding being too broad or vague in the problem's cause and solution. It is also essential to focus on how the problem and solution align with the grantmaker's interests while avoiding ancillary information from the Assessment. Keep in mind: One program or project can have more than one intended impact, especially if it is a multi-pronged endeavor; one program/project can address more than one need in the community. Stay focused on the funder's alignment with the Needs Statement.

The purpose of the Needs Statement is about the cause and need. The grant proposal's purpose is to close the funding strategy gap for a specific program/project or other budget essentials. The cause and need are derived from the Needs Assessment. The gap is derived from the funding strategy and committed support. The gap is calculated this way:

Total Program/Project Budget - Secured* Funds = Funding Gap

(*Funds that are awarded or collected, not funds that are pledged or pending.)

Now that the purpose of a Needs Statement is understood, how is one written expertly? One analogy to help get it right is a great gorge between two mountains, with a river flowing through it. The cause is the flowing river that eroded the earth away, forming the canyon.

The need is to stop the river from flowing and creating a more significant divide—the gap between the sides of the gorge had to be bridged. The grant funding is the bridge connecting Point A (one side of the gorge on which constituents are "trapped") to Point B (the other side of the canyon, where respite and change await). The Needs Statement is a word picture created about the relentless river creating greater need the longer it is not slowed or stopped. A sense of urgency is conveyed by the partially completed bridge leading to the other side—partially completed because only a portion of the required funds have been secured, and the grantmaker can finish bridging the gap.

It is compelling for the grantmaker to finish bridging the gap, impacting the positive change. The Needs Statement frames the grantmaker as the hero of the story. Storytelling is getting the audience to listen to and see themselves as part of the story. Compelling storytelling in grant proposals validates the audience's humanity by supporting the request with facts, figures, and testimonials. The need should logically resonate in the funder's mind because it focuses on why the problem exists in the community.

A Needs Statement can compel by being as short as one paragraph or as lengthy as eight to ten pages. The scope of the problem, type of funding, size of the ask, the bottom line of the budget, and capacity of the organization dictate the length of the Needs Statement. The typical Needs Statement is from one to three pages. Let's consider what goes into creating the Needs Statement.

As referenced, a Needs Assessment provides the information from which the Needs Statement is written. An assessment is a process of gathering and discussing information from multiple and diverse sources to understand a situation or condition. Therefore, a Needs Assessment involves evidence from numerous and varied trusted resources supporting the existence of the situation or condition addressed by the nonprofit's mission. This evidence should be quantitative and qualitative, including statistics from relevant and reliable sources, facts and figures from recent studies (recent is relative to the data and research available), and applicable testimonial and anecdotal evidence. The sources should be cited for proper attribution as well as a later reference for clarification, if necessary; it helps to know from where the information came.

The Needs Assessment should be wide-ranging across all nonprofit areas, not limited to the information for a single grant proposal's Needs Statement. A Needs Statement is required in most grant applications. About two-thirds of the Needs Statement's work happens in the Needs Assessment. However, the efforts exerted to create the Statement can benefit the entire organization. Areas of the nonprofit sourcing a Needs Assessment include:

- Program/project team for program/project development and evaluation by setting a tone of urgency
- Executive management for strategic planning, budgets, public relations and marketing, annual reports, and human resources decisions
- Board of directors for governance
- Accounting and finance for budget narratives and line item justifications
- Development and fundraising department for grant proposals, capital and annual campaigns, endowments, events, and more
- Volunteer coordinator for recruitment and retention of volunteers, in addition to anticipated volunteer hours required for organization activities
- Communications and marketing department(s) for content creation for public relations, media, social media, website, newsletters, and more.

Most Needs Assessments address the social determinants in the community contributing to the cause of the problem. Social determinants can include the education level of adults, food insecurity, affordable housing vacancy rate, eviction rate, lack of health insurance, homelessness, availability of health care services, violent crime rate, and unemployment. Statistics and research on these critical factors are easily researched. (The block covering "Research for Grant Proposal Content" offers a variety of resources.)

The Needs Assessment provides information supporting the logical argument for the financial partnership to attain program/project sustainability. Because the Assessment is long-range, it will likely show that the problem's cause can only be eliminated with systemic change, which is not a "one and done" task in most cases. Although the Needs Assessment is not a component of a grant proposal, it is integral in crafting a compelling and SMART

Needs Statement or Case for Support:

Specific—Use quantitative and qualitative research closely related to the organization's mission and activities, making a logical case for the intended outcomes and impacts.

Measurable—Employ facts and figures emphasizing the scope of the problem, scalable to the community.

Achievable—Structure cause(s) of problem and solution(s) with feasibility.

Relevant—Apply recent expert data and testimony.

Time-bound—Limit cause(s) of problem to relevancy within the community and a reasonable timeframe.

How is the Needs Statement crafted from the Needs Assessment? How can the Needs Assessment answer, "Why should you care? Why now? Why us?" in the grantmaker's mind? Storytelling. The story is composed with a focused, fact-based narrative supported by comparative, current, relevant, cited statistics and trends. It is complemented by compelling, honest storytelling with a tone of urgency. And the moral of the story, so to speak, is that the story must not only directly connect to and support the organization's ability to respond to that need in the community but directly align with the grantmaker's focus and purpose for funding. Storytelling in the Needs Statement does not include individual stakeholder stories, however.

Being a prolific writer is not a skill required for great storytelling in Needs Statements. Knowing the elements of tried and true storytelling is obliged, and recognizing where these elements are found in the Needs Assessments is crucial. The tried and true storytelling elements are setting, characters, plot and conflict, resolution, and the (happy) ending. For the Needs Statement, extract this information from the Needs Assessment to extricate the Nonprofit Elements of Storytelling:

- ✓ Setting—Physical location in which problem exists (area, community, city, state, region, country) OR current situation or condition
- ✓ Characters—Group receiving services OR Inputs (human, financial, and physical/tangible resources)
- ✓ Plot and Conflict—Description of the problem addressed by the organization's

mission, programs/projects, and the cause(s) of the problem
- ✓ Resolution—Create experiences leading to outcomes through activities and outputs
- ✓ (Happy) Ending—Impacts (long-term change) experienced by the character(s)

After identifying the elements in the Needs Assessment, the writing is mechanical.

1. Write phrases and sentences depicting the physical location where the program/project or other funding need exists. The physical location can be a building, community, specific neighborhood, or group within a community or a region. In contrast, the setting can be a situation or condition that exists. Many Needs Statements benefit from utilizing both settings.
2. Write phrases and sentences describing the characters—demographics, characteristics, expected numbers of the group receiving services OR list the inputs. For longer Needs Statements, it is likely to have both sets of characters.
3. Write phrases and sentences explaining how the intended outcomes involving the characters address the mission through the program/project or other funding gaps. The Needs Statement implicitly or explicitly talks about the problem(s) and the underlying cause(s) by addressing the mission.
4. Write phrases and sentences highlighting activities, outputs, and outcomes of the program/project and making logical connections between them using quantitative and qualitative examples. The logical connections portray progress towards the impacts and explain how the characters are positively impacted. This exemplifies improvement in the setting as well.
5. Write phrases and sentences illustrating the intended impacts—the fundamental changes anticipated as a result of the program/project, including the long-term benefits of the program/project. Impacts should be quantified whenever possible. (A word about Impacts: There are no right or wrong impacts.)

After writing phrases and sentences supporting the ask for grant funding, polishing the prose is next. The polishing process connects to the heart and highlights the hurdles. Polishing combines phrases and sentences with transition words, relationship words, and conjunctions to strengthen the language that compels giving. Polishing tactfully and strategically inserts adjectives, adverbs, and action words, enhancing the original phrases and sentences. Polishing takes advantage of editing and proofreading for succinctness and proper use of writing conventions. An unexpected benefit of polishing is that it can help significantly adjust to word or character count restrictions in applications. Transitions and conjunctions effortlessly reduce words and characters in first-draft forms of phrases and sentences. (All of the tools for complete and compelling storytelling are provided in the block on "Storytelling for Grant Proposals.")

Heart-centered connections are effortlessly made when the content is humanized. Choose one or two authentic storylines featuring how or why funding the gap for this program/project or other organizational penury betters a living thing that has been diminished or damaged. There are a variety of stories a nonprofit has to tell. Some of these are the founding story. A historical perspective with a "walk down memory lane" and overcoming adversity. Donors, volunteers, board members, and partner perspectives ascertained in the Needs Assessment are equally informative and articulate the nonprofit's vision.

Although individual stories are not recommended in Needs Statements, the history and anticipation of outputs, outcomes, and impacts of those stories evoke emotion. However, most importantly, connecting a "face" with an impact is not exploiting those receiving services. Some participants appreciate sharing their stories. It connects heartstrings. People fund people (or other living things like puppies or the environment), not programs/projects. And grantmakers are people.

Highlighting hurdles might sound counterproductive when asking for money. However, most nonprofits do not have unique missions or programs/projects with outputs and outcomes that do not overlap with others in the community. Part of the solution is clearing the hurdles of the past. The Needs Statement should communicate the current situation or condition of the community and what it can be in the future if the solutions are implemented with the proposed funding. The barriers preventing the previous resolution of the problem could support this edict. The heartstring connections and highlighted hurdles are crucial to creating a tone of urgency. They are also integral in squelching, "So what?" as the grant proposal reviewer finishes reading an application. A lack of urgency translates to a lack of return on their investment.

The completed Needs Statement should resemble the logic model in content. Reviewing from the block on "Logic Models for Grant Proposals," logic model development eliminates much of the narrative of program/project planning. The logic model shows the plan; the narrative tells the story. Much of the information in a logic model can be used for Needs Statements. The Needs Statement is also a foundation for Program/Project Descriptions and Program/Project Evaluations.

It is obvious why Needs Statements are one of the most critical components of a grant proposal. That is why it is imperative they be SMART. Ensuring that all grant proposal components emanate a cohesive message strengthens the ask and adds to the nonprofit's credibility. SMART guidelines for Needs Statements are:

Specific—Use quantitative and qualitative research closely related to the organization's mission and activities, making a logical case for the intended outcomes and impacts of the grant funding ask.

Measurable—Employ facts and figures emphasizing the scope of the problem, scalable to the community; includes expected benchmarks during and after delineated time.

Achievable—Structure cause(s) of problem and solution(s) with realistic feasibility based on the organization's capacity and target population interest.

Relevant—Apply recent expert data and testimony significant to outputs and expected outcomes and impacts.

Time-bound—Clarify how the grant award will help achieve the organization's mission and funder's focus during a particular stated period.

Needs Statements are sometimes the section of the grant application with the fewest words. Regardless of the number of words or pages, it sets the tone for the rest of the proposal. It bears repeating: Stay focused on the funder's alignment in the Needs Statement.

Program/Project Descriptions for Grant Proposals

The program/project description is the discourse intended to provide an image of what is to be implemented with inputs and experienced by the target constituency. On the one hand, most people can put the sentences together that explain the why, what, how, who, where, and when of a program or project—to write a description. On the other hand, most dread doing it, and some simply hate it and are not comfortable doing it.

Before we learn how to craft a well-written description, I want you to understand the difference between a program, a project, and activities. Most nonprofits have programs, not projects. Programs focus on achieving the mission (which addresses a need in the community). Programs do not necessarily have a specified length or deadline for completion but are executed to obtain the mission's impacts continuously. However, program budgets and evaluations typically have a set timeframe, usually a calendar year or the organization's fiscal year. Note that the grant funding acquired for a program/project does have an end date typically during which the money should be used to achieve outcomes and impacts agreed to by the terms of the proposal submitted.

A project can be independent of a program, or a set of (related) projects can complement one another and align in a logical sequence to create a program. Projects are often part of a program, distinct, and implemented for a specified duration, possibly with the desired result tied to the mission but not directly supporting the mission. Most grant proposals are submitted for program support but can indeed be submitted for project support. Understand that many grant applications for individuals, especially in the arts, are submitted for projects. The same holds for for-profit grant funding and grants for home improvements.

Activities take place to implement programs or projects. A set of activities can combine to form a program or project. Grant proposals in the nonprofit world are not solely submitted for funding to support activities. The cost or expenses of activities are included in the program/project budget and typically do not require funding independently.

Do not use any of the three terms interchangeably. Regardless of what it is called, it is crucial to be consistent with verbiage in grant proposals. Too, using the terms correctly will bolster credibility, improving the chances of securing grant funding for the program or project. Let's look at how the three terms remain distinctive in grant proposal narratives, including the Program/Project Description:

A program is one or a set of projects linked together and executed sequentially to attain combined benefits for the mission. It focuses on context, operates on a long-term or ongoing timeframe, is strategic in nature, produces outcomes, and can be grant-funded.

A project is a temporary but structured activity undertaken to create a distinct product or service for specific outputs, directly or indirectly supporting the mission. It focuses on content, operates in the short-term, is technical or tactical, produces outputs, and can be grant funded.

An activity is an action or event using inputs (resources), and when combined for implementation, results in outputs and outcomes for program or project impact(s). It focuses on using resources for specific purposes, operates in the immediate and short term, is technical or tactical, contributes to outputs and outcomes, and is typically not grant-funded on its own.

In our example program, Flip It Reverse Job and Career Fair is a program of Mentoring Individuals with Disabilities organization. In the program design, the Resume Reboot, Let's Talk About It, Display Board Build, Dress for Success, Employer Forum, and Wrap-up are the program's activities. In this particular program design, they are not projects because their outputs benefit the outcomes. Even though these activities are short-term, they are not conducted or evaluated for independent impacts in this particular program. A different organization could choose to make each of these activities separate projects.

To help distinguish between an activity and a project in the program design, ask 1) if the activity is being conducted as part of a program whose elements are evaluated and reported independently or if it is being conducted to evaluate and report the outputs of all activities as a whole and 2) how the purpose of implementing the activity relates to the mission.

1. For example, in the program Flip It Reverse Job and Career Fair, the purpose of conducting the Let's Talk About It Mock Interview workshops is to improve job applicants' interview skills and comfort level when talking one-on-one with strangers. In this particular organization, there is no reason to conduct mock interview workshops on an ongoing basis; therefore, the activity does not qualify as a program.

2. For this particular program, the number of attendees for the Let's Talk About It workshop, along with voluntary, self-disclosed demographics, including gender, race, or age, will be tracked. This data will not be used for analysis beyond showing that job seekers participated in the workshop, nor will it be used in scope or scale for the program's impact(s) analysis. The program's success is based on the number of job seekers with disabilities getting a job offer, not how the mock interviews impacted getting the job offer. Therefore, the mock interview workshop is not a project.

3. Because the activity does not qualify as a program or a project, it must be an activity and handled as such in a program description for a grant proposal. A different organization might want to use the data for different or more analytical purposes, perhaps qualifying the activity as a project or even a separate program.

We know that the mission and program/project are derived from the need, and in the grant proposal writing world, need stems from a living thing being diminished or damaged. Therefore, by explanation, the program/project description tells the world that the organization will use funds most prudently because it identifies specifics about the who, what, when, where, why, and how of a program/project that addresses those diminished or damaged. But how is that communicated? How are the why, what, how, who, where, and when described succinctly and compellingly? It is communicated through the details—through the description. It is communicated through storytelling.

Describing the program/project seems simple enough: Tell about what is necessary to achieve the intended impact(s):

- Who—the staff, volunteers, partners who will help execute the program/project, and target group(s) received services or benefit from products
- What—the inputs and activities compulsory for the expected outputs, outcomes, and impacts by executing the plan that addresses the mission
- When—the anticipated timeframe in which the community change happens or the expected time frame necessary for the target group(s) to receive services or benefits from products
- Where—the physical location can be a building, a region, a city
- Why—the evidence-based need in the community that addresses the mission
- How—the resources and activities required to create the outputs and outcomes, and implementation

These are the details. A description is an oral or written representation of the details, usually in narrative form. For grant funding, it is a written representation: We use these inputs (resources) for these activities to produce these outputs (results) so that the stakeholders experience these outcomes (ways in which change is experienced), leading to these long-term or permanent positive impacts (effects). Each *these* will be a list of its relevant program/project details. Rather than replacing the word *these* with a list and having that very long sentence suffice as a program/project description, tell a story with narratives that incorporate evidence, charts, tables, infographics, and storytelling. Writing compelling descriptions takes practice. It is the balancing act of combining the mundane prose of evidence-based program/project details with language that builds the lump in readers' throats.

The program/project description is linked to the Needs Statement. Both should be rooted in evidence. You know your community has a need for your program/project; that alone is not enough to convince grant funders that the program/project truly addresses a need and is sustainable, making it worth their investment. Evidence is the facts and information, often proven by other authorities, indicating what you believe to be true about your community has validity. Incorporating evidence shows homework has been done towards creating a sustainable program/project and that it is not a whim. Evidence can be shown in narratives, charts, tables, and infographics. Evidence can be qualitative or quantitative.

The program/project description should strive to meet several evidentiary benchmarks:
- Solidly affirm that the organization is action-oriented to the need(s) of the community
- Steadfastly upholds the organization is an authority on the subject
- Actively seek partners and collaborations for funding and program/project implementation
- Directly work toward SMART impacts
- Closely relate the program/project and activities to the budget and logic model, tying them to the organization's sustainability and program/project

Compelling storytelling is the ultimate function of an effective program/project description. Regardless of word count, descriptions should get in and get out without taking the reader through a rhetorical maze while meeting the referenced benchmarks. Even when restricted by character counts, descriptions cannot leave the reader wondering how the program/project fulfills its mission or why it is implemented. For the best-selling novelist, storytelling is perfected by using tried and true elements of storytelling; the same is true for grant proposal writers. For now, it is necessary to know why storytelling is critical to successful grant applications. Creating good storytelling with the tried and true elements of storytelling will be learned later. (Storytelling for grant proposal writers is explained in great detail in the "Storytelling for Grant Proposals" block.)

Be SMART with Program/Project Descriptions:

Specific—Identify explicit resources and activities for implementation.

Measurable—Characterize quantitative benchmarks of participation and activity levels for expected outcomes and impacts.

Achievable—Do not seek to change the world, only address change needed or anticipated in the community.

Relevant—Pinpoint the resources and activities to accomplish the outputs, outcomes, and evaluation(s).

Time-bound—Isolate a timeframe for the benchmarks to be executed and completed.

Why aren't sentences about the who, what, when, where, why, and how enough to convince a grant proposal reviewer to make the investment? Loosely linked sentences usually do not tug at heartstrings. They might accurately identify those receiving services and characterize the intended outcomes and impacts, but descriptions need to evoke emotion to compel action—the action of awarding the grant. The standard information (who, what, when, where, why, and how) is elevated through integrating tried and true storytelling elements—setting, characters, plot and conflict, resolution, and happy ending—to evoke emotion. This probably sounds more like creating content for an annual report, year-end appeal, 990 narratives, or community impact report. The versions are inextricably linked, but the program/project description includes evidence of need. In contrast, the content for public relations includes more data and metrics from the program/project results. Writing compelling program/project descriptions with word or character restrictions takes practice too.

Compelling descriptions do not use much technical talk or jargon. Keep the language relevant, however. Too much jargon can confuse the message or give the impression that the need or implementation of the program/project is not fully understood. Some use of terms directly relating to the program/project and area of service is necessary, but rewriting the White Paper or dissertation from which evidence was gathered is not storytelling. An expert in the field can review that content for accuracy and clarity in your narratives in the draft stages. (Money can be included in the budget to hire a professional to help create narrative and budgets for technical aspects.)

The word description evokes ideas of flowery prose, layers of text, or droning speeches. Just because the word *description* is used for this grant proposal component does not mean that it has to be all words or narratives that confirm the earlier referenced benchmarks. Charts and tables can be powerful communication tools. They can go far in clarifying confusing or juxtaposed information. They are also useful to break up paragraphs or pages of content by providing a change in style or format and adding some extra white space for the reader's eye.

The title of the program/project should be evocative too. While a name should not be "cute," alliterations, meaningful acronyms, and subtitles can grab attention and arouse curiosity. A program/project title should never be a question.

Leveraging evidence-based program/project descriptions will significantly strengthen grant proposals by balancing authority and emotion. They also demonstrate sustainability, explicate evaluation methods, justify reporting, and set the organization ahead of the competition. Perfect the balancing act of combining the mundane prose of evidence-based program/project details with language that builds the lump in the throats of readers for the most effective grant proposals.

Tarra Nystrom

Program/Project Evaluations for Grant Proposals

"We know we did the program. We know we didn't spend any money on anything unnecessarily. The clients are happy. We're done!" Not quite so fast. Don't you want to know the level of success of the program? How and to what degree was the community improved? The grant funder wants to know! The program/project is pointless without understanding if anything changed for the target constituency for better or worse. Only through evaluation can there be an understanding of any change. Evaluation determines the value, nature, character, or quality of something or someone; it is an assessment.

Program/project evaluation is a part of the grant process from application to post-funding period reporting. For program/project funding, a grantmaker almost always wants to know how the organization will know if the intended impacts occurred or are near the expected levels, and if not, why. They want to see how the program/project will be assessed to determine the level(s) of success. The process and evaluation methods are typically part of the program/project design and separate from the Program/Project Description. The grant proposal writer can be a great asset to the nonprofit's team by helping the program/project manager understand the evaluation information a funder wants to see and how to construct the evaluation format.

Traditionally, the task of program/project evaluation (assessing impact) falls on the program/project department. The problem is that a program/project team is primarily concerned with delivering services, not analyzing how the program/project affects the participants or community. Because the grant proposal writer is charged with understanding the grant award's funding guidelines, they know what deadline-driven information needs to be reported to the funder. Additionally, as the grant proposal writer or development director, grant funding reporting falls on you. Post-grant funding period reporting summarizes the use and implementation of inputs, activities, and outputs along with the resulting outcomes and impacts supported by the grant award. Corroborating this information with the program/project team for evaluation ensures the work of evaluating is done thoroughly, with no overlap, and tabulated only once. Although a grant proposal writer might not be directly responsible for the program/project evaluation, they should be involved with the process.

This block is intended to help you learn how the program/project evaluation figures into the grant proposal writing process, not teach how to create comprehensive evaluation plans. With that said, it is beneficial to know what comprises a quality evaluation for a program/project, including two all-encompassing steps:

1. A systematic and consistent collection process
2. Analysis of the information

The reporting is written from the information drawn from the analysis.

In essence, the systematic and consistent collection involves measuring all outputs, outcomes, and impacts, obtaining quantitative and qualitative data. Performance measures elicit a summary of indicators that answer whether the program/project is achieving or has achieved its anticipated marks. (The process and considerations to obtain this quantitative and qualitative data are explained in great detail in the block on "Data and Metrics for Grant Proposals.")

The analysis must discern if implementing inputs, activities, and outputs resulted in any change. It differentiates the intended or expected results (outcomes and impacts) from the unintended or unexpected consequences. It determines if how the results are revealed proves any change. When working with research metrics, one measurement means more or is more clearly defined when integrated with other measurements; all performance indicators should be measured for a more thorough analysis. Performance indicators are derived from outputs and outcomes. Suppose a measurement turns out to be irrelevant to a particular reporting parameter. In that case, it can be dismissed (but retained for other uses).

A logic model is helpful for evaluation and reporting, as well. The outcome evaluation makes it possible to anticipate the impacts. Remember, because the impacts are long-term, most post-award grant reporting will include the expected impacts—the impacts assumed from the evaluation of inputs, outputs, and outcomes, not actual quantified results. Using evidence-based program/project strategies will help make these assumptions more accurate. When developed thoroughly, all possible outcomes are inventoried in the logic model. It will show what to measure and determine how to measure each outcome by brainstorming in the planning process. Some performance measures will have only one way to be quantified or qualified (i.e., evaluated). Others will have multiple ways to assess their benchmarks. Depending upon what information is rooted in the collection process, the strength of links between outcomes and impacts, or lack thereof, can be established through analysis. If the links are weak from the output(s) to outcome(s), that specific outcome might not need to be evaluated at all; that outcome can still be included in the logic model. Remember, the inputs and activities make up the planned work; the outputs, outcomes, and impacts represent the intended results.

By accepting grant money, you most likely agree to report to the grantmaker about the program's success concerning inputs, activities, outputs, outcomes, and impacts—the ways in which the return on their investment is explained. These explanations are drawn and written from the analysis step.

If grant funding is awarded for non-program/project expenses, the reporting typically does not involve evaluation but rather a report of purchases and uses promised by the proposal. Receipts are evidence of promises kept. To elevate this reporting, a concise narrative of how the new equipment, staff training, or capital improvements have improved operations and increased efficiency is an appropriate addition to the balance sheet or scanned receipts.

The management of grant money also should be SMART, which includes Program/Project Evaluation and Reporting:

Specific—Were the identified explicit inputs and activities implemented for the program/project towards achieving anticipated outputs, outcomes, and impacts defined in the grant proposal for logical analysis?

Measurable—Was quantitative information for all performance measures collected? Was qualitative information for all performance measures collected?

Achievable—Were the inputs and activities executed for expected outputs, outcomes, and impacts within the scope of community need and scaled within the nonprofit's capacity per the Program/Project Description and Budget(s) submitted with the grant application? If the measurement itself is difficult to understand, then it will lack validity and transparency.

Relevant—Did the information collected provide adequate analysis to determine if a change occurred with regard to the problem identified in the Needs Statement and reflect the needs of all stakeholders?

Time-bound—Was the data collected and analyzed in a timeframe that maintains information integrity and relevance?

Evaluation and reporting for grants might look different than the evaluation and reporting conducted in the organization. The grant proposal writer's responsibility is to understand the grantmaker's reporting requirements, even if they do not directly align with the nonprofit's. Regardless of how their reporting parameters align or make sense to you, they are the reporting parameters agreed to when submitting the grant application.

It is not disputed that evaluation and reporting take time and, therefore, staff hours. At a minimum, payroll dollars are associated with performing program/project evaluations and producing a report. Some organizations opt to hire research firms to analyze the program's results. Again, more expense to accommodate the obligation. Interestingly, many grantmakers allow 5-10% of the total program/project budget to be designated for evaluation.

So much of securing funding for nonprofits relies on storytelling. The grant process's Evaluations and Reporting component does not rely on that compelling combination of heartstring-tugging and clever presentation of facts and figures. Clean, concise narratives combine with simple, easy-to-understand tables for Program/Project Evaluation and reporting in the grant process. And before submitting the report to the grantmaker, ensure that all data and analysis are included as offered in the grant proposal AND the funder's guidelines.

Metrics are dreaded. Narratives are daunting. And deadlines are stressful. But how else can we gauge if what we planned and hoped for came close to reality? It is natural to fear the evaluation and reporting processes based on a natural reaction to writing about data and metrics when facing a deadline. For grant evaluations and reporting, the process is purposeful, revealing, and consequential to the sustainability of the mission as well as programs and projects. Understanding that the process does not require an advanced degree in research and analytics will alleviate the dread.

Budgets for Grant Proposals

If, when asked whether or not you have a budget, your answer is, "No," you are not grant-ready. Period.

A budget is not prepared for the grant proposal. It is required information in a proposal. If no budgets are created, how can you possibly know where your funding gaps exist? Budgets are a bitch, and they are dreaded because most of us are not accountants or even "numbers people." You do not create a budget for the sole purpose of including it in the grant proposal. This planning step should be done long before the grant proposal is started. Remember, budgets are not the same as financial information. Budgets are a snapshot of costs, while financials are historical information on what was spent and how well the money is managed. Budgets should be SMART:

Specific—Identifies explicit line-item budget items necessary to implement a program/project or execute organizational operations.

Measurable—Expenses are attributed to inputs to implement the activities.

Achievable—Expenses and revenue are realistic and appropriate for the efficient use of donor dollars.

Relevant—Budget items are directly related to the program/project that addresses the community's need and the nonprofit's mission.

Time-bound—Budgets are set for a program/project period (typically 12 months, unless otherwise described) or for one fiscal year of the organization.

Budgeting is a necessary evil for running any business entity, especially a nonprofit organization. Budgeting demonstrates thoughtfulness and planning. It helps to establish the organization as an authority regarding its mission. Because the board of directors should approve every budget that the executive management has prepared with input from key staff, budgets show board engagement and oversight. Budgets link program/project descriptions to the implementation—the resources crucial for all activities that, when executed, result in expected outputs, outcomes, and impacts for a set timeframe. Each program/project has a separate budget, and when combined with the general operating and fundraising budgets for 12 months, it results in the organization's annual budget.

A budget is an estimate of income and expenditures for a set period. In the nonprofit world, there is more than one budget showing the necessary revenues and expenses to keep the doors open. There are organizational budgets, operating budgets, program/project budgets, and fundraising budgets for annual and multi-year timeframes. A capital campaign might have a separate budget or be integrated into the fundraising budget. The majority of grant proposals require a yearly program/project budget. Some funders ask for an annual organizational budget as well. If the grant funding ask is for multiple years, a complementary multi-year budget might be required.

Budgets in grant proposal writing, like budgets for all things, link money with outcomes. A budget and a grant proposal make a case for how much money is allocated to achieve the purposes of the funder's focus and the organization's work. Dollar figures, as well as narrative sections, are compulsory in most grant applications. The narrative is the justification for the dollar values in the budget. Any budget can be updated (never changed) throughout the funding period.

A project/program budget is a list of expenditures often categorized to support achieving the program/project outcomes. This is a line item budget with a total amount for each category, such as personnel (salaries), fringe benefits directly related to the personnel, travel, equipment, supplies, software, technology, and anything else required to implement the activities. A program/project budget might include a percentage of indirect costs, such as building rent, utilities, and administration salaries, if the grant allows for funding indirect costs. (As a clarification, if a grant excludes salaries or operating costs, but you can demonstrate that other funding covers those expenses, do not eliminate the opportunity. Simply clarify how their money will not be used for expenses precluded in the proposal because other funding streams cover them.) The evaluation process of any program/project can incur costs; funders often allow nonprofits to designate up to 10% of the total project budget for evaluation.

There are different types of budgets. The organization or department may have a master budget, operating budget, cash flow budget, program/project budget(s), or financial budget. It can be confusing. In the nonprofit world, the master budget is the same as the organizational one. A functional budget is a tool to show expenses and revenue of a limited area of a company, a particular program/project, operations, or other nonprofit areas. The word "functional" does not mean that the budget works or balances. Instead, it applies to a function, department, division, project, or other specific aspects of the business. A functional budget is usually unnecessary for standard grant proposals for nonprofits, for-profit companies, or arts or writing projects. Although usually not required in addition to a program/project budget, a functional budget is essential to being awarded and managing grants because they best show the gap between the budget and the already secured funding. Even if one is only used internally, it is good to create one. However, federal, state, or local government grant proposals might require a functional budget because it provides additional detail to each line item. Each line item is linked to achieving a particular organizational function, such as fundraising, each program/project, or capital endeavors. A functional budget is advantageous if various parts of the program/project might be funded by different funding or revenue streams within the organization, or perhaps if various grantmakers might fund multiple parts of a program/project.

Everything encompassing a program/project's execution must be addressed in the budget. Using the logic model is an excellent place to discern budget costs and items to be included from the column labeled inputs (resources). Anything required to make that activity happen should be considered in the budget—personnel, travel, equipment, supplies, building or other physical location, or contractual labor. The link between the list of inputs and the program/project budget is evident. Everything needed to implement the program/project must be allocated in the budget. However, the office supplies might be grouped as one line item and one input (resource)—the pens, legal pads, copy paper, and more to be paid for when implementing the program/project. The staff required to make it happen might include one full-time program manager, one-quarter time of the Executive Director (25% of their wages and fringe), three full-time employees, and administrative support for 20 hours per week (50% of their salaries and fringe benefits) and the total expenditure can be entered as one line-item (salary and wages) in a budget but as many as six inputs in a logic model, for example.

Take a look at inputs (i.e., resources): The human, financial, and physical resources that support the grant-funded project or program. These might include grant funding, cash, in-kind matching funds, staff and volunteer time, facilities, equipment, supplies, building or office, transportation, and community partners. Inputs are the tangible and intangible elements that go into the program/project, the ingredients aspect of a program/project's recipe for success. The list of what is considered an input needs to be inclusive and encompassing.

Everything required to implement the program/project and achieve outcomes needs to be in the budget, even the things with no direct cost or monetary requirement. Everything provided through in-kind donations and partnerships is necessary. Note that in-kind donations of goods and services are reported on the revenue and expenses of a budget, and they must equal each other.

Volunteer hours have a dollar value and can add significantly to a budget. Accurately reporting volunteer hours and their corresponding value demonstrates sustainability, community support, and efficient management. Grant reviewers know what is generally required to make a program/project happen. They have seen it all and will know if things are missing from the budget. That lack of transparency or carelessness can lead to distrust and not being awarded the funding the organization needs and deserves.

Providing budget information numerically and narratively offers an accurate snapshot of the grant partnership request. One way to accomplish this while creating sustainability and credibility is to list the secured and potential funding additional to the ask represented by the application being submitted. This can be done with a separate table or within the budget presentation.

Some notes about the sample budget displayed on the next page: Note that grant funding is no more than 20% of the budget; a suggested best practice is for a funding strategy to be up to 30%. Notice the Volunteer Value information is represented as Total volunteer hours multiplied by the Volunteer Value (a dollar amount) as set by the IndependentSector.org as of August 2022 in this case. Example: 50 hours x $29.95 = $14,975. Notice, too, that the value of volunteer hours is not included in the revenue total but is listed as a dollar value. These are fictitious grant funders.

Additionally, capital campaigns are not part of every annual budget. Therefore, no capital campaign money is included in this Funding Strategy example. (Capital campaigns are covered in greater detail in the "The Basics and Beyond" block.) It is ok if the Expenses and Funding sides do not balance. In our example, they do. Let's look at a sample budget:

Budget: Flip It Reverse Job and Career Fair	
Expenses	$$$
Job fair venue	800
Venues—Resume Reboot, Tell Me About It, Dress for Success, Display Board Build, Employer Forum, Wrap-up	0
Supplies and equipment	1,260
Transportation stipends, mileage reimbursement	400
Website	94
Bottled water, healthy snacks—all events	65
Salaries—program manager	12,295
Fringe benefits	0
Disability inclusion handbooks	1,184
Utilities, office space	0
In-kind goods and services	1,735
TOTAL	17,833
Funding Strategy (Revenue)	$$$
Grants	8,500
Weisenberger Family Foundation	5,000
Rolston Pipe and Tool Grant Program	3,500
Association for Disability Employment	2,000 (pending)
Human Resources Professionals of Ohio	1,000 (pending)
Sponsorships	3,923
In-kind donations	1,735
Private donations	3,674
TOTAL	17,833
Volunteer Value = 50 x $29.95*	14,975 value

Unfortunately, it is not enough to use just what the accounting department puts in the shared file. Grantmakers feel the need to read even more narrative. The budget narrative provides another opportunity to demonstrate transparency, accountability, and sustainability. Following are examples of budget narratives:

A. "Mentoring Individuals with Disability's business office, program manager, and grants manager work together to ensure that all grant awards are utilized according to the terms and conditions of the grant agreement and that all grant reports are completed and filed on time."

B. The venue for the job fair is provided for $800.00, a 50% discount on the rental rate. The ancillary workshops' venues are provided at no charge through our partnership with the Columbus Metropolitan Library system.

C. Budgeted office supplies and portable electronic equipment for all activities total $1,260.00. Additional supplies and equipment are provided through a $1,435.00 value of in-kind donations.

D. The mileage reimbursements and transportation stipends, crucial to job seekers being able to participate, total $400.00. Bus passes totaling $200 are included in the $1,735 in-kind partnerships total.

E. The Flip It Reverse Job and Career Fair dedicated website facilitates information, registration, reminders, and education for program participants, hiring managers and business owners, and volunteers at the cost of $94.00.

F. Everyone benefits from healthy snacks and bottled water free of charge at all job and career fair events. The estimated expense is $65.00 and does not include an additional partnership of $100.00 in-kind grocery gift card to offset other snack expenses.

G. Salaries total $12,295.00 for the Program Director currently overseeing the program and will spend 50% of their time coordinating the Flip It Reverse Job and Career Fair. This individual's annual salary is $24,590. There are no fringe benefits associated with this salary.

H. Ongoing disability inclusion education and training are provided to job seekers, hiring managers and business owners, and volunteers through a printed handbook, The Disability A-Player Plan: Employee of the Month Every Month, for a total of $1,184.00.

Narratives can be formatted in various ways (bullet points, paragraphs, sections) but should always be written in complete sentences.

The Cost Per Unit of Service (CPUS) can be included in budget narratives to suggest the funder's investment value. Here is an example: "The Cost Per Unit of Service is budgeted at $185.76 for each job seeker with disabilities to secure integrated, living wage employment to reduce reliance on public services, improve self-esteem, and contribute to local and national economies." The Cost Per Unit of Service for a particular program/project is calculated by dividing the total program budget by the number of (actual) participants:

Total Budget / Total Participants = Cost Per Unit of Service

$17,833 / 96 = $185.76

For budgeting, the expected number of participants is the only number available for calculation. Historical data touts the efficiency and sustainability of the program/project and is aptly included in budget narratives. Using the actual number of participants in historical reporting of Cost Per Unit of Service data (rather than the anticipated number) increases the cost per unit (intuitively, increasing the amount of money needed to implement), but few programs/projects realize 100% forecasted participation and is the only way to report this information accurately. Therefore, a false narrative about the true need would be created.

The Cost Per Unit of Service is complemented by a cost revenue analysis to make a case for awarding grants. Explicating how a budget line item such as software or technology reduces the Cost Per Unit of Service is persuasive: "A one-time investment of $12,000 for software will streamline the job development process for job seekers with disabilities, reducing the Cost Per Unit of Service from $185.76 to $115.35." The potential funder understands that the organization will use all donor dollars more efficiently. This benefit can be communicated in budget narratives, Program/Project Descriptions, and Evaluations.

Consider cost revenue analysis as:

CPUS + Impact = Cost Benefit

Sometimes the funder requires the applying organization to provide matching funds or a proportion of the total program/project cost so that the funder is not paying for everything. The availability of these matching funds must be clearly stated in the budget and budget narrative as already committed to the program/project; they cannot be hypothetical or something that will be found once the primary funding is secured.

For those who are not adept in accounting practices, direct and indirect costs can be points of confusion. A grant proposal writer does not need to become an expert on a glossary of accounting terms, but understanding these two types of costs will be worthwhile. Direct costs are incurred specifically for the implementation and success of the program/project. Every line item in the program/project's (board-approved) budget is a direct cost. Indirect costs are incurred for common or shared objectives, not solely for the program/project implementation. An indirect cost cannot be readily identified with a particular final cost objective. Most administrative expenses are indirect costs. Examples of indirect costs are utilities and rent expenses, health insurance, equipment depreciation, officer salaries, human resources, accounting and legal fees, or office and cleaning supplies.

DIRECT COSTS = directly for program/project
INDIRECT COSTS = everything else that makes operations possible

Shared costs can figure into organizational budgets and proportionately allocated to program/project budgets. A shared cost is one that benefits more than one accounting area, usually more than one program/project. When in doubt about the percentage used by one or the other area, allocate the entire shared costs as an indirect cost. Direct costs correspond with program/project inputs, and indirect costs include expenses that do not quite fit neatly into a program/project budget.

Although variable costs and fixed costs are not typically listed on budgets submitted with grant applications, it is vital to be familiar with them. They are sometimes confused with direct and indirect costs by those not trained in accounting. Variable costs are usually program/project-oriented. They vary in size, amount, degree, or nature from something else of the same general class and change from one condition, form, or state to another. For example, a program/project number of participants or timeframes of the services might change from year to causing the costs to be revised from a previous budget. The costs will change because of the inputs required to change with varying program/project changes. Fixed costs are not affected by programs/projects. As a reminder, some examples of fixed costs are permanent staff, rent/mortgage, and principal and interest payments on long-term loans. Executive staff, rent, and loan obligations will not change even if the program/project costs change.

In essence, there can be direct variable costs and indirect variable costs as well as direct fixed costs and indirect fixed costs. Let the accounting team and board's finance committee handle the minutia of these finer budget details.

Do not get bogged down with the tug-of-war between wages and salaries as administrative costs and administrative costs are indirect costs (which are usually not funded by grants). More and more foundations are funding wages necessary to run the program/project. They understand that volunteers do not run most programs/projects. Be transparent and honest about salaries and fringe benefits for employees, including contracted labor expenses allocated proportionately in the program/project budget. A good rule of thumb is if a program manager's time is allocated 100% to one program/project, then 100% of the salary and fringe are included in the corresponding budget; if 25% of an organizational administrative assistant's time is dedicated to the program/project, then 25% of their wages and fringe are included in the corresponding budget. An executive staff member can be directly involved as a program/project input, mostly in smaller nonprofits where the staff wear multiple hats. In this case, the wages and fringe proportionate to the percentage of their time dedicated to the program/project should be part of the budget.

Salaries, and therefore fringe benefits, are most often miscalculated. The size of the nonprofit can be linked to these miscalculations. An internal audit of how much time is spent on activities related to the expense categories will help estimate indirect costs. In a small nonprofit, the Executive Director (ED) prospectively will devote more time to program/project services than an ED of a large organization, who will likely spend more time on management tasks. Similarly, in a small entity, the person fundraising or writing grant proposals (a prong of fundraising) might also devote time to program/project activities. The percentage of a particular employee's salary or wages must be budgeted in indirect costs accurately. Consistently, the percent of the employee's fringe benefits must be calculated and budgeted precisely in indirect costs.

Some grant guidelines clearly state that no salaries or wages are allowed. This indicates a restriction on how the money is allocated if the grant is awarded. Even though the budget includes human capital that typically gets paid a salary or wages, and it is evident that the program/project cannot be implemented without personnel, some funders want their investment allocated to only supplies, equipment, and other tangible inputs (resources). If the guidelines or instructions do not preclude any specific costs, then assume it is appropriate and allowable to include personnel expenditures necessary for the program/project in the grant ask. The list of budget line items to be funded is contingent upon the funder's guidelines. In these cases, the budget must still include the salaries, wages, and fringe benefits, but the other appropriate component(s) of the grant proposal shows a clear understanding of and agreement to adhere to the guidelines.

A next-level budget presentation showing the potential funder their guidelines a fully understood looks like this budget form below. Hypothetically, the grant guidelines stipulate no salaries or fringe benefits can be covered by this (restricted) funding. The ask is $1,600.

Budget: Flip It Reverse Job and Career Fair		
Expenses - Detail	Total $$$ Program Budget	Total $$$ Requested from [grantaker]
Job fair venue	$800	$200
Venues—Resume Reboot, Tell Me About It, Dress for Success, Display Board Build, Employer Forum, Wrap-up	$0	$0
Supplies and equipment	$1,260	$600
Transportation stipends, mileage reimbursement	$400	$100
Website	$94	$0
Bottled water, healthy snacks—all events	$65	$25
Salaries—program manager	$12,295	$0
Fringe benefits	$0	$0
Disability inclusion handbooks	$1,184	$675
Utilities, office space	$0	$0
In-kind goods and services	$1,735	$0
TOTAL	17,833	$1,600

The concept can be easily adapted to show any budget item total and the funder's disbursement, not solely for salaries and fringe benefits.

The word overhead is frequently a source of contention and confusion. Most non-accountant nonprofit professionals use the terms indirect costs and overhead interchangeably. Just know that accountants and CPAs define indirect costs differently than how they define overhead, but for budgeting conversations and grant proposals, the terms are transposable.

Overhead or indirect costs are considered to include administrative costs such as accounting expenses, insurance, building maintenance, utilities, and the salaries and fringe of administrators. Like grant applications, definitions of indirect costs might not always look the same to any two organizations, even though they should be. For the sake of consistency and transparency, the IRS Form 990 (the nonprofit tax return) classifies expenses into three categories:

- Program/project Services Expenses
- Management and General expenses
- Fundraising expenses

From these categories, indirect costs are calculated by adding Management and General expenses to Fundraising expenses and dividing that total into the total expenses.

(Mgt. & Gen. $ + Fundraising $) / Total $ = Indirect Expenses or Overhead

To exemplify:

Program/project Services expenses = $160,000

Management and General Operating expenses = $30,000

Fundraising expenses = $10,000

TOTAL expenses = $200,000

$30,000 + $10,000 = $40,000 / $200,000 = 20% Indirect Costs or Overhead

Charity raters use the IRS categories to affirm indirect costs for an organization in their rating systems. This is important to grant proposal writing because funders are likely to look at charity ratings and the 990 as part of the grant review process. It is crucial for budgets to report direct costs/indirect costs correctly. An inaccurate number can present significantly higher indirect costs or appreciably lower actual program/project costs. Neither poses a good situation.

An incomplete budget can be detrimental to the organization but also a grant ask. Suppose only the line item expenses are presented in the budget. In that case, there is a missed opportunity to reveal thoughtful planning and sustainability through in-kind donations of goods and services, volunteer value, and additional funding partnerships and fundraising. Why is this important to grant proposals? If the line items to implement the program/project total $136,790, and the ask is $50,000, the ask represents 37% of the budget. In addition to the line items, assume that in-kind contributions are $34,560, volunteer hours valued at $2,856, additional secured grants total $26,000, and other donations total $16,350, the total program budget is now $216,556. The $50,000 ask is only 23% of the total budget. Less than one-quarter of the budget versus a little more than one-third is a safer investment for a prospective grant funder.

It is the grant proposal writer's responsibility to submit accurate budgets in grant applications. However, it is most likely not their responsibility to create the budgets. Providing accurate budgets does require understanding the organization's operations and program/project activities well enough to identify inaccuracies and missing budget items. Budgets for grant proposals should be SMART:

Specific—The budget of the program/project or other funding gap is closely tied to the grantmaker's focus and guidelines.

Measurable—The budget items are realistic and evidentiary to what is necessary to implement the program/project.

Achievable—The budget, budget narratives, other proposal narratives, and logic models are complementary and demonstrate the feasibility of success for the program/project or other funding gaps.

Relevant—The budget's items are directly linked to the implementation and success of the program/project or other funding needs.

Time-bound—The budget accurately shows expenses for the funding period or other demonstrative requirements in the grantmaker's proposal instructions.

So, what should that accurate, well-presented budget look like for a grant proposal? First and foremost, the budget needs to be presented in a clean, neat table with an easy-to-read font, font size, and spacing. Creating a worksheet in Excel or table in Word provides some flexibility for formatting. Here are some tips:

- Other than an outside frame to the table (a box), hide the lines separating rows and columns for a neater presentation with white space. It is easier on the reviewers' eyes. Maintain the same font and size as the rest of the grant application—Times Roman, Arial, and Tahoma at 12-pt are good options; do not size the font any smaller than a 10.
- Clearly title the budget with the organization's name, program/project name if appropriate, and the date range that the budget encompasses.
- Include column headings using bold or italicized typeface to differentiate titles from the information.
- Check the math and recheck it.
- Check the math again.
- Use whole numbers, rounding numbers to the nearest whole dollar for more effortless reading: $.01 to $.50 round down, $.51 to $.99 round up.
- Align figures correctly and consistently.
- As always, save the final budget as a PDF for attaching to a proposal or email.

The best grant proposals are accompanied by expense-driven budgets created with reasonable and allowable expenditures. However, the most emotive, illustrative Mission Statement, Needs Statement, or Program/Project Description cannot replace a solid fiscal foundation. The budget represents the basic building blocks of that foundation. Approximately 30% of grant reviewers look at the budget first. Make it count.

Financials for Grant Proposals

Financials foment fear. Pulling together financial information can be time-consuming, frustrating, polarizing, and even paralyzing. Remember, financial information is not the same as budgets. Budgets give a snapshot of what it costs to implement programs/projects or operate the organization overall in a given period. Financials are historical information about what was spent and how the money is managed. Fear-mongering or not, transparency and completeness of financials translates to increased funding from all funding streams, recent research shows.

What documents are considered financial information for grant applications? Income statement(s), balance sheet(s), and audited financials are all on the table. Whether internal or external, the accounting team can provide the grant team with the required documents. The executive staff is also a resource for the most current and accurate financial documents. Financial documents should always be submitted as PDF files with grant proposals. The grant proposal writer must be familiar with each.

An income statement focuses on the organization's revenues and expenses during a specified period. Income statements come with various monikers. The most commonly used are "Statement of Income," "Statement of Earnings," "Statement of Operations," and "Statement of Operating Results." Many professionals (especially on the for-profit side of business entities) still use the term P&L, which stands for profit and loss statement; however, this term is seldom found in print now. Additionally, the terms profits, earnings, and income mean the same and are used interchangeably.

A balance sheet is a statement of the assets, liabilities, and capital of a business or other organization at a particular point in time, detailing the balance of income and expenditure over the preceding period. It is a statement of a company's financial position at one specific moment in time. This financial report shows the two sides of an organization's financial situation—what it owns and what it owes.

A financial audit is the professional opinion of an outside Certified Public Accountant (CPA) serving as an auditor on the material accuracy of an organization's fiscal year-end financial statements. The auditor is hired and paid for by the nonprofit. An audit has nothing to do with the financial strategy or viability of the organization. Too many nonprofit staff, board members, and funders believe that a clean audit opinion implies financial health. In reality, a clean audit opinion merely states the financial statements accurately reflect the organization's true financial health, good or bad.

Audited financials opine a nonprofit's close adherence to policies, procedures, and standardized best practices with financial records, accounts, business transactions, accounting practices, and internal controls of a charitable nonprofit by an independent auditor. "Independent" refers to the fact that the auditor/CPA is not an employee of the nonprofit but is retained through a contract for services. Therefore, they are "independent."

The IRS does not require nonprofits to obtain audits, but federal and state government agencies do, depending on the nonprofit's size or spending. An independent audit is not the same as an IRS audit. Instead, it is an examination of the accounting records and financial statements by an independent auditor. At the conclusion of the examination, the auditor issues a report in the form of a letter stating whether, in the auditor's professional judgment, the nonprofit's accounting records and fiscal year-end financial statements fairly represent its financial position according to Generally Accepted Accounting Principles (GAAP). The auditor's letter is attached to the front of the financial statements.

The benefits of an audit include generating donor (including grantmakers) and constituent confidence, ensuring compliance with accounting standards, and preventing or discovering fraud.

Having audited financials should be the aspiration of every nonprofit. However, audits are expensive and might not make financial sense for smaller organizations. An audit is generally unnecessary for small nonprofits because they engage in a low number of financial transactions each year. The veracity of their books can be checked in a less expensive way—a review.

In a review, a CPA examines the financial records. This examination is less thorough than a full audit. It differs because the CPA does not offer an opinion on whether the records follow GAAP guidelines. During a review, the CPA examines the financial statements but does not consider the nonprofit's internal controls (typically included in the scope of an independent audit). Instead, the review provides a limited level of assurance that the financial statements are free of misrepresentations. The CPA concludes whether they are aware of any material modifications for financial statements to conform to GAAP. A review costs about half as much as a full audit and should never be referred to as an audit.

What if the organization has no formal audit or review? There are policies and procedures to demonstrate fiscal responsibility and transparency when adopted and approved by the board of directors. These policies and procedures (which also speak to sustainability) detail how financial records are maintained, designate authority and hierarchy of controls, assign authority to spend (approve purchases), and demonstrate a well-structured system for tracking restricted contributions and how they are expended in real-time. Copies of these board-approved practices, with a date stamp of approval, often can be submitted with financial statements in lieu of an audit or review. Additionally, the IRS Form 990 can strengthen funder confidence when consistently reviewed by the finance committee and board of directors, submitted on time, and completed taking full advantage of governance question responses, program/project descriptions, and other opportunities for narratives. The 990 postcard that nonprofits with annual revenue under $50,000 can file does not substitute for a full 990 when bolstering financial responsibility and transparency. A quality community impact report can be produced annually also. In demonstrating impact and accountability, an annual report is an effective marketing and donor cultivation vehicle that can reinforce the nonprofit's commitment to financial transparency; it can be submitted with or as an attachment to grant proposals. A comprehensive budget free of jargon and acronyms will also demonstrate fiscal efficiency and transparency, along with fiscal year-end financial statements for at least the two most recent years prepared in accordance with standard accounting practices.

As noted earlier, it might not make financial sense for some organizations to perform an audit or review. A general rule for conducting an external audit or review includes organizations with operations over $250,000 annually. For smaller organizations with budgets between $50,001 and $250,000, internal financial statements and fiscally responsible best practices will suffice for grant applications. Many organizations with budgets under $50,000 are scaling up to have the capacity for grant awards but should also operate with fiscal responsibility and transparency from the start. (As explained in other blocks, start-up and smaller organizations are eligible for and win grant awards by articulating evidence-based need and program/project design, comprehensive evaluation processes, and thorough budgeting.)

Financials submitted with grant applications need to be SMART:

Specific—Provide financials for only the number of years indicated in the grantmaker instructions; if the number of years is not defined, assume it is the most recent fiscal year.

Measurable—Grantmakers can ask for any number of financial reporting periods and scope of financial information they deem appropriate for their review process that quantifies the organization's condition and sustainability.

Achievable—Grantmakers can ask for any number of financial reporting periods and scope of financial information they deem appropriate for their review process, supporting the nonprofit's success in addressing the mission.

Relevant—Financials are directly related to a program/project that addresses the community's need and nonprofit's mission and speaks to the efficient and transparent policies and procedures set forth for the nonprofit.

Time-bound—Financials are prepared for a program/project period (typically 12 months, unless otherwise described) or one organization's fiscal year. Grantmakers can ask for any number of reporting periods and scope of financial information.

Financials inadvertently speak to the nonprofit's capacity to meritoriously deliver the program/project. Although historical, the information ascertained by the grantmaker through financials carries equal weight as budgets, evidence of needs, and programming innovation.

Executive Summaries for Grant Proposals

An Executive Summary is merely capturing everything about the organization or program/project on one page! No problem. An Executive Summary is the first (and perhaps only) impression made for an entire grant proposal. Obtaining the right balance of evidence, emotion, edict, and expression is not achieved in a single draft of this grant proposal component. And as referenced in other blocks in this book, the purpose of this one is not to teach you how to write the perfect Executive Summary but to inform about its relevance in grant applications.

First of all, an Executive Summary is one page. One page, 8.5"x11" with one-inch margins, including four to six paragraphs, and is written for the program/project or organization, not as a Cover Letter or historical synopsis. In some grant guidelines, the Executive Summary is referred to as an abstract. An abstract is found more with government and academic grant guidelines than foundation guidelines. The Executive Summary has little to do with summarizing and more to do with selling. For grant proposal writing purposes, the Executive Summary is to sell the solution for the community's problem for which the nonprofit established its mission. It focuses on the benefits offered by the program/project rather than features; the features are featured in the grant proposal's body. The Executive Summary may be the only page of the proposal considered before the reviewer flips to the budget.

Anecdotally, I learned very early as a writer to compose the introduction to an article, report, or academic paper last. This sounds counterintuitive, I know. Although an introduction can serve as an outline for the rest of the piece, the content often veers from the original path, causing at least a partial rewrite of the introduction. The system of writing it last also keeps new information from being introduced in the proposal's body that does not show up in the introduction or the case of a grant application, an Executive Summary. Think of the Executive Summary as the proposal's introduction. There will be a better idea of what needs to be said and how it should be said by scripting the Executive Summary last after the program/project description, evaluation methods, and budget narrative are complete. A new Executive Summary is not written for every grant application. It is written once and updated as appropriate after periodic reviews. If one is not a required component, be sure to use it in the attachments to a proposal.

Ensure the scripted summary is relevant for grant proposals. An Executive Summary includes an opener, the need, the solution, the evidence, and a call to action. Two or three critical points from key components are identified to integrate into the Executive Summary content. These points should be found in Organizational Information, Needs Statement, Needs Assessment, Program/Project Description, Program/Project Evaluation components, and key impacts from the Logic Model. Rephrased, the Executive Summary should mention two or three of the most important points elaborated on in the Organizational Information, Needs Statement, Needs Assessment, Program/Project Description, and Program/Project Evaluation sections.

Parts of the Executive Summary, associated content, and the content's origin/critical points comprise these ideas:

- The Opener grabs attention with an energized, action-oriented introduction of the organization's mission and program/project. The Organizational Information and Program/Project Description are suggested critical point areas from which to create a strong opener.

- The Need evokes emotion through demonstrating a solid understanding of community problem(s), including cause(s). The Needs Assessment and Needs Statement are suggested critical point areas from which to write about the need.

- The Solution persuades with primary, secondary, and tertiary impacts through inputs, activities, outputs, and outcomes. The Program/Project Description and Evaluation Methods, as well as key impacts from the Logic Model, are suggested critical point areas from which to convey an innovative solution.

- The Evidence concretely supports the Need as well as the primary, secondary, and tertiary impacts. The Needs Statement, Needs Assessment, and other research are suggested critical point areas from which to explain the evidence-based components.

- The Call to Action indirectly invites (funding) partnership by broadly expressing the ROI of the funder's investment. A conclusion emphasizing benefits, not features, and integrating the suggested critical point areas of the Program/Project Description, key impacts, and the Needs Statement completed the Executive Summary.

A well-written Executive Summary will make the organization's grant proposal submissions SMARTer:

Specific—Expertly written for a particular program/project or organization (not for a specific grant application)

Measurable—Competently includes quantitative and qualitative evidence and expected outcomes and impacts

Achievable—Confidently speaks to the likelihood of successful implementation and completion

Relevant—Cogently addresses the community need and cause

Time-bound—Comprehensively incorporates timely evidence (three years); consistently reviewed and updated periodically

A well-written, compelling Executive Summary can be used as a one-page appeal to condensed grant proposals or other fundraising activities, including sponsorship packets.

As shown in the sample at the end of this block, the Executive Summary takes advantage of the skill of writing concisely without jargon or technical language. It elaborates on the solution and evidence, not the problem or cause. Because the Executive Summary is one of the first things a reviewer reads, ensure it is persuasive and compels them to continue reading the grant proposal. This component demands comprehensiveness and brevity. The following is an example of a SMART Executive Summary:

Executive Summary

MENTORING INDIVIDUALS WITH DISABILITIES PROPOSES TO INCREASE THE RETURN OF INVESTMENT ON DISABILITY INCLUSION

Mentoring Individuals with Disabilities(MIWD), 501(c)3, is looking to increase the already fervent support from disability agencies and the business community in order to provide this innovative mentoring experience by creating greater familiarity with the Return on Investment (ROI of disability diversity in the workplace. The experience helps job seekers with disabilities develop the necessary skills and experiences they'll need to compete in today's competitive workforce while assisting area companies in securing some of the most dedicated employees in the Columbus, Ohio market.

While the unemployment rate for people with disabilities recently was reported at its lowest in three years, the Allsup Disability Study: Income at Risk reports that people with disabilities experienced an unemployment rate nearly 65% higher than the rate for people with no disabilities in the second quarter of 2018. As a result of MIWD, this employment inequity will be reduced as individuals with disabilities will:

- Increase earnings and earning potential
- Increase the likelihood of securing health care benefits
- Increase self-esteem. self-worth, and independence
- Increase inclusion through social and professional opportunities
- Reduce dependency on public and private vocational rehabilitation programs

Mentoring Individuals with Disabilities assists individuals with disabilities with person-centered job development activities for sustained, competitive employment. The program connects employees of varied physical and mental disabilities with employers through career exploration experiences at local businesses interested in diversifying their human resources recruitment on an ongoing basis. Mentoring Individuals with Disabilities Day underscores the impacts of the ongoing program pursuits. MIWD Day is a community-awareness building event held quarterly, focusing on sustainable, competitive employment for individuals with disabilities. MIWD seeks to match mentees/job seekers) with area businesses offering job shadowing and hands-on career exploration. Additional informational events are provided in October, National Disability Employment Awareness Month.

Employers have the opportunity to conduct the Americans with Disabilities Act (ADA) and disability etiquette training for management and employees in their workplace as part of this program because familiarity and knowledge eliminate barriers. Employers are provided with extensive ROI of Disability information and marketing support to display in the workplace. Mentees are matched on a first-come, first-served basis in areas of their vocational goals and interests. A reception celebrating the event will be hosted at the end of the workday, honoring our mentees, mentors, business partners, sponsors, and volunteers.

The combination of the Mentoring Individuals with Disabilities programs and Mentoring Individuals with Disabilities Day allows MIWD to apportion awareness that despite the additional obstacles that people with disabilities confront, they want to work and earn a sustaining, living-wage income.

Partnerships, Volunteer, and In-Kind Donations Information for Grant Proposals

Even if you could go it alone, you shouldn't. Partnerships, volunteers, and in-kind donations keep a nonprofit from going it alone while providing oft-overlooked support for grant proposals. If contributions, tangible and intangible, are not tracked, those receiving services are being shortchanged along with the staff, board of directors, donors (including grantmakers), and community.

In the nonprofit world, we hear the word partnership quite often. Partnerships are fundamental and expected, especially by funders. By definition, a partnership is a formal arrangement by two or more parties, usually involving close cooperation having specified and joint rights and responsibilities. Between nonprofits, partnerships can range from formal and detailed agreements to causal, "handshake" accords. Regardless of the structure, partnerships and collaborations augment efficiency, leverage funding, increase outcomes and impacts, and unite the community. Be SMART about partnerships and collaborations:

Specific—Logical partnerships fill gaps to strengthen all stakeholder experiences for more effective program/project implementation. Partnerships are most effective when they benefit identified specific needs for the community and partner organizations or provide increased outcomes and improved impacts by combining resources and efforts.

Measurable—All collaborations should benefit the bottom line in some way, quantitatively every time and qualitatively whenever possible.

Achievable—Partners boost the accountability of results (outputs, outcomes, and impacts) because they hold one another to task via formal or informal agreements. Establishing partnerships can increase the capacity for the success of the program/project.

Relevant—Because all partners in the program/project should have a vested interest, shared resources and activities are advantageous for all involved. Relevancy of partnerships will build upon existing strengths and create a competitive advantage.

Time-bound—Partnership agreements typically set parameters to have activities occur in a delineated timeframe.

There are a variety of partnerships that can be forged between and within organizations. For grant award purposes, partnerships indicate a cooperative organizational culture, services-centric policies and procedures, community impact awareness, and pragmatic use of funding. These all are indicators of sustainability that can be quickly reported to grantmakers. Do not collect partnerships for the sake of a list. Connections are made based on common ground and understanding. Partnerships must be intentional and not transactional.

For grant proposals, there are many types of potential partnerships: Civic groups, faith-based organizations, government agencies, community foundations, academic institutions, businesses (all types and sizes), consultants and sub-contractors, other nonprofit organizations, and internal departments and teams.

A list of partnerships and collaborations should be maintained and reviewed periodically. It is helpful for grantmakers to know what role a partnership plays in the program/project or other funding needs, not just their name. Include a brief explanation with the name of each partner. For example:

MIWD Partnerships
Fiscal Year 20**

Partner	Product, Service	Purpose
Center City Job Agency	Referrals; partner for community events	Shared inputs (personnel); activities
Fred's Sub Shops	Sandwiches, chips, and beverages for 9	Monthly board meetings
Printers 'r Us	Copiers and printers	Equipment and operations; Resume Reboot workshops

Do not confuse the presentation of this list as a table with a logic model. This is an inventory with explanations; there are no logical connections.

Another list of partnerships is funding partners, particularly grant funding partnerships. This inventory is vital to telling the funding story, which influences a grantmaker's decision. The decision to contribute to the program/project can be prompted by:

- Demonstrated prudent management through a diverse funding strategy (i.e., no more than 30% grant bursary)
- Enhanced credibility through additional grant awards promoted by the context of, "If ABC Foundation gave $15,000, the investment must be worthy of my money." Proven program/project and organization sustainability through ongoing and varied grant strategy included in diverse revenue planning.

Partnership information can be communicated in several grant proposal components, such as partnerships, budgets, sustainability statements, funding strategies, or other appropriate sections either in the application itself or in the attachment(s).

Grantmaker partnerships should be highlighted separately from other collaborations. Accurate representation of those funds being awarded/secured or pending Is prudent and expected. Because less than 20% of grant requests are awarded, an application for which no decision is known cannot be considered awarded or secured. It is pending. Transparency is essential when touting these types of partnerships, as demonstrated in the MIWD Grant Partnerships graphic below:

MIWD Grant Partnerships
Fiscal Year 20**

Grant Partner	Amount	Status
City of Columbus	$50,000*	Secured
		*2-year grant
		$25,000 - 2020
		$25,000 - 2021
Weisenberger Family Foundation	$5,000	Secured
Rolston Pipe & Tool Grant Program	$3,500	Secured
Association for Disability Employment	$2,000	Pending
Human Resources Association of Ohio	$2,000	Pending

Remember, the total secured grant funding should be no more than 30% of the total program/project budget. It is reasonable to show that grant funding for more than 30% of the budget is pending because fewer than 20% of grant requests are granted. In this case, pending means that the application has been submitted, and no decision has been advised. Pending means that the grant opportunity is on the Grants Tracker, an application has been submitted, but the award decision has not been announced.

Further evidence of partnerships and collaborations presented with grant proposals are Letters of Support and Memorandum of Agreement (MOA), also referred to as a Memorandum of Understanding (MOU). A Letter of Support can be written by a partner—faith-based, civic, social, corporate, philanthropic, government, consultants, or academic. These supportive and contractual documents are used to forge cooperative work relationships on an agreed-upon purpose or meet an agreed-upon objective. Providing a copy of the agreements (if not required) as an attachment is common sense in grant proposal writing.

SMART reporting of partnerships includes:

Specific—Detail partnerships specific to the programs/projects, administrative tasks, fundraising, or other activities for which they are used.

Measurable—Identify quantitative and qualitative partner information and data.

Achievable—Keep collaborative commitments and expectations realistic to organization operations and activities.

Relevant—Partnerships are established for tasks or activities to achieve the mission. Do not enter into partnerships for the sake of a list.

Time-bound—Partnership agreements (formal and informal), activities, and accomplishments should be evaluated consistently and periodically.

Volunteers do partner with nonprofits, but their contributions are valued differently than other partnerships and in-kind donations. Many nonprofits could not operate without volunteers. And many nonprofits do not realize the benefits of volunteers beyond imparting "manpower." Volunteers performing administrative duties often are experts in their area of volunteer services, such as accounting or graphic design, saving the organization money on contracted services or staff hours. Data entry probably does not require an advanced skill set, but it can save many staff hours, translating to payroll savings and affording employees time to accomplish other tasks. The "manpower" contributions of volunteers are invaluable. Period.

The time and talents volunteers bring to nonprofits go beyond the obvious. Volunteer hours have a dollar value associated with them. Independent Sector is recognized as an authority on volunteer value. At the time of this book's publication (late 2020), each volunteer hour's national average value was $27.20; the value was $29.95 by August 2022. State-level information is available at no charge on the Independent Sector website. Because there is a monetary value to volunteer efforts beyond the multiple additional benefits, every nonprofit must track every volunteer hour. This data is more critical for organizations applying for grant money.

The measure of volunteer hours is advantageous to grant proposals. If the Flip It Reverse Job and Career Fair estimates using 460 volunteer hours in 2022, the dollar value is (460 x $29.95) $13,777. In many nonprofits, $13,777 is close to the equivalent of at least one part-time program/project employee or more. Volunteer hours should be integrated into every program/project and additional administrative tasks throughout the organization whenever possible. Incorporating chunks of volunteer hours in which businesses, civic groups, and community associations can participate in the volunteer plan is a win-win. Volunteer Time Off programs are increasing in popularity in small and large businesses. Partnering with companies that provide this benefit has multi-pronged remunerations for the nonprofit.

Volunteer Value can be calculated for a program/project, administrative tasks, or department-specific reporting over a specific period or annually. The dollar value of each volunteer hour changes year to year. If previous years' totals need to be computed, consult IndependentSector.org's data for that year. Volunteer management software easily tracks hours and purposes (program/project, admin tasks, departments). Usually, it offers logs for volunteers to self-report accurately.

Volunteer hours X Dollar Value per Volunteer Hour= Volunteer Value
Total # Hours x Hourly Value Rate = Volunteer Value 460 X $29.95* = $13,777
(*$29.95 was the value of a volunteer hour in August 2022.)

For grant funding purposes, volunteers demonstrate responsible management, represent matching dollars, confirm community engagement, and exhibit collaboration. When appropriate, leverage an increase in volunteer usage in a comparative statistic to bolster program/project sustainability. In grant applications, emphasize the skills and knowledge that volunteers contribute to the program/project and overall organizational operations in budget and other narratives, infographics, and charts. Be sure to mention any special training in which volunteers participate that improves outcomes and impacts. Convey the dollar value of volunteer hours in budgets, as well as in terms of savings to the nonprofit's payroll or other expenditure items. Images of volunteers in action are powerful storytelling tools in relevant attachments. (Be sure to obtain proper releases/permissions to use those photos.) SMART Volunteer Tracking is crucial for grant funding:

Specific—Track volunteer hours specific to the programs/projects, administrative tasks, fundraising, or other activities for which volunteers are used.

Measurable—Identify quantitative and qualitative volunteer data.

Achievable—Keep volunteer commitments and expectations realistic to organization operations and activities.

Relevant—Volunteer hours should be kept to a reasonable amount for tasks or activities; do not inflate reported hours or overschedule for the sake of total hours.

Time-bound—Track hours daily, weekly, and/or monthly based on volunteer shifts; reconcile regularly and consistently, reporting to all internal partners and applicable external partners.

The value of in-kind donations adds up quickly and, like partnerships and volunteers, indicates cooperative organizational culture, services-centric policies and procedures, community impact awareness, and pragmatic use of funding. In-kind donations include tangible supplies, technology, equipment, software, food and beverage, event space for programs/projects or fundraising, vehicles, or waived vehicle rental charges. They are non-cash contributions. The value of the manpower, such as volunteers to process in-kind donations, is not considered an in-kind donation. All in-kind donations should be recorded and assigned an average fair market value. If Paul's Pizza provides four pizzas and six two-liter sodas for the quarterly board meeting, then the hypothetical in-kind donation would be tracked as (4 x $11.95 per pizza) + (6 x $1.99 per two-liter soda) = $47.80 + $11.94 = $59.74.

There is a differentiation between an in-kind donation of professional services and a volunteer or board member providing professional services. Here is an example: If a contract needs reviewing and an attorney who has no other connection with the organization waives the fees associated with the service for which an invoice would be issued, it is reported as an in-kind donation. In most cases, if a volunteer or a board member provides that professional service related to their regular work/career but does not charge for the service, it is considered volunteer time. In such cases, all organization by-laws, policies, and procedures must be followed concerning any compensation, conflict(s) of interest, or any other situation outlined in by-laws, policies, or procedures. State and other laws where an organization is located might dictate how non-paid professional services are handled.

Be aware of any guidelines or laws explicit to the organization's services about required or appropriate in-kind donation reporting. One example is food pantries partnering with a food bank as part of the food bank's consortium/approved agencies. Typically, there are strict guidelines on how purchases and non-cash contributions are figured into budgeting and program/project design. Grantmakers are astute and will know if in-kind donations for the identified services area align or not.

In-kind donations can be made voluntarily by external parties or solicited on the nonprofit's behalf. A nonprofit is not obligated to accept every in-kind donation offered. For example, Mentoring Individuals with Disabilities would never use a commercial refrigerator and would then be tasked with re-gifting the donation. Do not collect any in-kind donation for the sake of a donation. Be SMART and strategic:

Specific—Track in-kind donations to the programs/projects, operational, fundraising, or other activities for which in-kind contributions are made.

Measurable—Identify quantitative and qualitative in-kind donation information.

Achievable—Program/project, operational, capital, fundraising technology, and more in-kind solicitations should be within the scope of purpose and usability as well as the capacity of the organization.

Relevant—In-kind donations should only be accepted and solicited for direct use by the organization.

Time-bound—Track in-kind donations daily, weekly, and/or monthly based on organization demands; reconcile regularly and consistently, reporting to all internal partners and applicable external partners.

Maintaining accurate records of partnerships, volunteer hours, and in-kind donations is crucial to grant proposal writing because having access to up-to-date information optimizes proposal content regarding matching dollars, community engagement, diverse support, and sustainability.

Attachments for Grant Proposals

Attachments might seem mundane, but attachments can make or break a grant ask. Dictionary.com describes an attachment as 1) an act of attaching or state of being attached; something that attaches, 2) an additional or supplementary device, and 3) a feeling that binds one to a person, thing, cause, ideal, or the like; devotion. It is easy to understand the value of attachments to grant proposals when thought about in these terms.

The first part of the explanation is an act of attaching or the state of being attached. In our digital world, attachments are commonplace in emails and online events such as webinars, virtual summits, online workshops, shared document platforms, and more. The act of attaching is simply uploading the desired document(s) to the platform for submission or sharing. The attachment(s) will often be attached in an email or uploaded to the grantmaker's online platform for grant proposals. Do not rely on links to documents within a grant proposal as a substitute for an attachment. Links do not always open as intended when copied, can be broken if the content is moved or changed, and other technological anomalies can occur.

The second part of the explanation states that an attachment is an additional or supplementary device. What is a supplemental device to a grant proposal? It is a document external to the application, regardless of the format or process of submitting the application. It is a device that connects, in concept, like a bridge. The content of the attached documents is typically not part of the content required in the proposal's various other components. Much of this information necessary for grantmakers to understand the program/project and the amount of money being asked is best viewed as a PDF, Word/Excel document, or infographic. Some of this information cannot be copied into an online application and remain in the format created initially for the best interpretation. The most common attachments are budgets, financial statements, and sponsorship materials.

There is an array of content and formats to be used as attachments to supplement application components, enhance understanding, demonstrate sustainability, and tell the story. There is a learning curve to knowing what to attach, how much to attach, and why to attach.

The third part of the explanation is not as evident as the other two: a feeling that binds one to a person, thing, cause, ideal, or the like; devotion. Isn't this what we attempt to do in other fundraising activities? It makes sense to do this with grant proposals. Attachments provide an added opportunity (beyond storytelling in the other proposal components) to create empathy for those receiving services and benefitting from the program/project. Attachments should not be an afterthought.

Attachments offer a further opportunity to connect with the funder and should be carefully considered and created. Do not include every brochure or every photo of volunteers. Instead, think about what information supports the ask and consider what visuals connect the data and metrics to those served. Be SMART about the attachments:

Specific—The attachment content supporting the ask is clearly defined and targets the grant funder's focus.

Measurable—The attachment content features outputs, outcomes, and impacts in narratives, infographics, and charts explaining qualitative and quantitative information.

Achievable—The attachment content is tied to the success of the outcomes, outputs, and impacts, demonstrating what inputs were used prudently to implement activities and accomplish outputs, outcomes, and impacts as close to expected, or why not if the mark was missed.

Relevant—The attachment content is closely connected to and appropriate for the ask. For example, a sponsor packet is not pertinent to government grant funding (in most cases).

Time-bound—The attachment content, in general, should be no more than two (2) years old; older statistics and stories can be used only if relevant, and no other resource is available.

Any grant funder can request information and attachments about anything pertaining to their investment of grant money. So, how might this list of most common requests look?

- IRS Letter of Determination

- Conflict of Interest Policy
- Nondiscrimination Policy
- Diversity, Equity, Inclusion, and Access (DEIA) Policy
- Technology Use Policy
- Financial and Budget Information and Documents, including narratives for organization and/or program/project
- Letter of Support, Testimonials, Award Letters
- List of Collaborations—(project) partners, sponsors, donations, in-kind contributions, including volunteer hours
- Marketing collateral—Brochures, FAQs, media, press releases, website
- Lists of inventories—capacity building, unrestricted, operating grants Other requests might include:
- Documents from State Organization/Incorporation Background/history
- Mission Statement
- Needs Assessment and/or Needs Statement (also known as Case Statement)
- Program/Project Description
- Program/Project Sustainability Statement and/or Plan
- Organizational Executive Summary
- Program/Project Executive Summary List of Key Staff
- List of Board of Directors and their Affiliations
- Resumes/Bios of Key Staff and Board of Directors Members
- Program/Project Evaluation Methods
- List of Strategic Partnerships, including event and program/project sponsors
- List of additional funding, including pending and in-kind (organizational and program/project lists)
- Letters of Support
- Memorandums of Agreement/Memorandums of Understanding (if any)
- Code of Ethics

- Financial Management Policies and Procedures
- Participant, partner, or volunteer testimonials
- State incorporation documents
- Sponsorship benefits or packet

Many times, the number of attachments is limited. Many other times, what to attach is dictated. There is nothing to be done about either. However, if there is a limitation, be strategic in what is in the attachment(s). Take advantage of creating a PDF, when possible, to send information and visuals that support the ask and have not been included in the other components of the application. Multiple files can be combined into one PDF for attaching. One suggestion is to combine documents for a total of six to eight 8.5"x11" pages using a combination of the organization's annual report summary, annual community impact report, client stories, volunteer testimonials, services-oriented infographic, an Executive Summary, a photo or photo collage, marketing martial(s), letters of collaborative support and partnership, or a Cover Letter. Be strategic about the order in which these varying documents are combined for visual acuity and prioritization of importance in supporting the grant.

Attachments can make or break an application. Although they are often the last step in the submission process, they should be considered with the same care and priority the other components are given.

Logic Models for Grant Proposals

Repeat after me, "Logic model." Now breathe.

Logic models unnecessarily evoke fear and anxiety when, in fact, they can be a powerful tool for a variety of planning and actions throughout a nonprofit organization, including the grant process. Forethought and details are necessary for programs, staffing, volunteers, budgets, funding strategies, and more within a nonprofit. Planning usually involves a collection of lists that gradually combine into program/project descriptions, staffing policies, volunteer initiatives, budget items, and a comprehensive blueprint of how the money will be raised. Planning is a logical process for success.

For many, the utterance of "logic model" conjures thoughts of complicated schemes of boxes of jargon and buzzwords with arrows pointing in several directions that often backtrack or skip seemingly illogically. And for some, this is what a logic model is precisely and should be. This is NOT our logic model. In the nonprofit world, our logic model describes how a program/project should work, presents the planned activities for the program/project, explains how the activities will be executed and documented, and focuses on anticipated impacts for targeted stakeholders. Our logic model in the nonprofit world is:

- A tool used to visually diagram the relationships between program/project goal(s), objectives, and expected outcomes
- A roadmap to steer the team(s), both internal and external
- A presentation of the concept of the program/project
- An example of intent; not reality

Logic models break down the cause-and-effect relationship between the program/project's activities and the change expected in participants receiving the program/project's intervention. Logic model development eliminates much of the narrative of program/project planning. The narrative tells the story; the logic model shows the plan. It generates a greater focus on the plan. Sometimes we can get too caught up in words (adjectives, adverbs, action verbs) rather than the plan itself. The words are very useful to other grant proposal components, however. Some of the benefits of logic model development include:

- Clarify program/project goals, objectives, and outcomes
- Identify assumptions and relationships between program/project efforts and expected outcomes
- Convey key components of the program/project
- Facilitate determining what to measure for evaluation throughout the program
- Promote self-correction

Keep breathing! These benefits will be explained thoroughly.

In nonprofit work, we have been trained to talk about goals, objectives, and outcomes. Goals and objectives are often confused with each other, and outcomes and goals are easily transposed too. In general, to clarify, a goal is a broad statement of what you wish to accomplish. Objectives represent steps towards achieving the goal. Outcomes are the anticipated quantitative and qualitative results to be realized by implementing or conducting the objectives. Note that a goal is only as good as the objectives that go with it. Planning is always built around "if-then" propositions, and objectives and outcomes are simply the "if-then" statements of the goal. "If we have volunteers, [then] we can hold the Flip It Reverse Job and Career Fair to help job seekers with disabilities who want to be working secure integrated, living-wage employment."

Program/project planning, whether narrative- or diagram-based, is a projection, an educated guess of what change can result from the community's well-researched need. Some anxiety about logic models might stem from our human desire to not want to be wrong and not let anyone down. Be assured that it is understood most programs/projects come close to their intended results, rarely achieving 100%. And most times, when the actual results differ from the intended ones, the two are not far apart. So as you plan, both narratively and through logic models, accept that they both represent the intention and neither represent reality. You will not know the reality until the program/project is completed when the "if-then" propositions are thoroughly evaluated.

Keep breathing!

Logic models are SMART planning:

Specific—Clarify the program/project goal, objectives, and outcomes (inputs, activities, outputs, outcomes, and impacts).

Measurable—Facilitate determining what to measure for evaluation throughout the program.

Achievable—Because they are a planning tool, the inputs, activities, outputs, outcomes, and impacts are attainable; and promote self-correction to ensure realistic expectations.

Relevant—The inputs, activities, outputs, outcomes, and impacts tie directly to the program/project or other funding gaps. Identify assumptions and relationships between program/project efforts and expected outcomes.

Time-bound—Identify requirements for a calendar, fiscal year, or another program/project cycle.

Before we jump into how to develop logic models, let's clarify some terminology and concepts. Program/project descriptions include goal(s), objectives, and outcomes for targeted stakeholders. Because logic models use related terminology (inputs, activities, outputs, outcomes, and impacts), I do not want you to get bogged down with confusion. Keep the end result in focus—a grant proposal that offers a concise and clear message about the goal, objectives, and outcomes requiring funding. You will use the logic model to explain the relationships of the goal, objectives, and outcomes (how's, why's, what's, when's, where's, and who's) of implementing the program/project in greater detail. The logic model will add the inputs (resources) and activities required to attain the goal and objectives (outputs), as well as convey the anticipated impacts of the outcomes. Let me repeat that. The logic model will add the inputs and activities required to attain the goal and outputs, as well as convey the anticipated impacts of the outcomes.

Five new words were introduced as a concept: Inputs, Activities, Outputs, Outcomes, and Impacts. A logic model details the inputs, activities, outputs, outcomes, and impacts that were more broadly labeled as the program/project's goal, objectives, and outcomes of the program/project. The two sets of terms are inextricably linked. Accept it. Embrace it!

THE TOOL –

Let's get comfortable with the idea that a logic model is a tool. A tool is nothing more than a utensil (a fork), a mechanism (the knob that, when turned, helps to open a door), a device (a computer or a hearing aid), or a whatchamacallit (the corner of a business card used to dislodge spinach from one's teeth). For nonprofits, a logic model is a valuable planning tool in addition to being a robust visual tool for grant proposals. In the physical instance that a logic model is a tool, think of it as simple as five boxes. The boxes represent the inputs, activities, outputs, outcomes, and impacts of a program/project into which you will drop pieces of paper (real, symbolic, or virtual) on which are printed the components and details necessary to implement the program/project. The five boxes are labeled inputs, activities, outputs, outcomes, and impacts.

Conceptually, each component of a program/project is written on separate pieces of paper. Each component will require components of its own—details. Details such as equipment, staffing, participants or stakeholders (perhaps with specific separate qualifiers), transportation, or supplies are part of the program/project components. We will address the details in more detail later. Consider writing these components and details in pencil, simulating the first draft because things will evolve and change! Some of the words or components will expectedly change. This is why it is called the planning stage. The basic logic model is an ideal planning tool. We will expand this basic logic model later, but for now, the basics are the best place to start.

Keep in mind that one program or project can have more than one goal, particularly if it is a multi-pronged endeavor. The need might require more than one way to solve the problem comprehensively. And although the expected impacts might differ, some of the inputs, activities, outputs, and outcomes might be the same for multiple impacts. Duplicate information is okay, as long as it is pertinent and appropriate.

In our working program example, there is only one goal: To assist people with disabilities who want to be working in securing integrated, living-wage employment. The overarching purpose is to plan and implement activities to increase the likelihood of the target group securing employment through improving interview skills and related proficiencies. An additional objective (i.e., activities and outputs) includes adding community partners to assist with activities and expanding employer awareness of disability inclusion in the workplace. The outcomes and impacts include integrated, living-wage employment for people with disabilities to reduce reliance on public assistance, improve self-esteem, and add disposable income to local and national economies.

To achieve the goal with its objectives and outcomes, you need the details. These are the details mentioned in an earlier section. Details are the inputs (resources) that will be used for objectives (activities), which will show the concrete indicators of the activities' results (outputs) along with their short-term benefits (outcomes). The long-term change (impact) or benefits are expected and/or reported from the evaluation.

Now forget the terms goals and objectives, and get comfortable with the idea of using the term outcomes in a more limited scope than you were accustomed to using.

Let me repeat that. Now forget the terms goals and objectives, and get comfortable with the idea of using the term outcomes in a more limited scope than you were accustomed to using.

What the heck does all of that mean? Breathe. It means that you are going to move from looking at a goal, objectives, and outcomes (as you probably more commonly refer to the components) to presenting them in greater detail through inputs, activities, outputs, outcomes, and impacts, making logical connections between the shared relationships among the five categories of details. It is essential to understand that submitting a grant proposal, in most cases, is for a new program/project or one that has had some changes from its initial implementation. Therefore, it is impossible to know everything about a program/project for sure. The actual inputs and activities are the only things known for sure. The outputs, outcomes, and impacts can only be estimated or projected. Here are the definitions of the details:

- Inputs (i.e., Resources) are the human, financial, and physical resources that support a grant-funded program/project. These include staff and volunteer time, facilities, equipment, supplies, building or office, transportation, and community partners. Inputs (resources) are the tangible and intangible elements that go into a program/project, the ingredients aspect of the program/project's recipe for success. The list of what is considered an input/resource should be inclusive and encompassing.

- Activities are what a program/project does with the inputs. Activities are the processes, tools, events, technology, and actions integral to the program/project implementation. These processes, tools, events, technology, and actions are used to bring about the intended program/project changes or results. In rare cases, the activities can be conceptual. This list lays out the actual activities that will occur as a result of the grant, such as workshops and training in the sample program.

- Outputs are the direct results of a program/project's implemented activities. These are concrete, quantifiable indicators of productivity. What can be quantified as a result of the program? How many people will be reached? How many will participate? What events will occur, and how many?

- Outcomes are the short-term and intermediate benchmarks for the target constituency during and after program/project activities. These are the short-term benefits of the program as opposed to the long-range, big-picture changes expected. Outcomes should be quantified whenever possible.

- Impacts are the fundamental change anticipated as a result of the program/project—the long-term benefits. The impact should be quantified whenever possible. (A word about Impacts: There are no right or wrong impacts. There are no right or wrong outcomes. Every program/project is different. Every organization is different, and missions vary. Do not compare your programs/projects to the competition or collaborators. Be confident in what YOU want to accomplish.)

**Inputs and activities make up your planned work;
outputs, outcomes, and impacts represent your intended results.**

Conceptually, you have five boxes, one each for inputs, activities, outputs, outcomes, and impact.

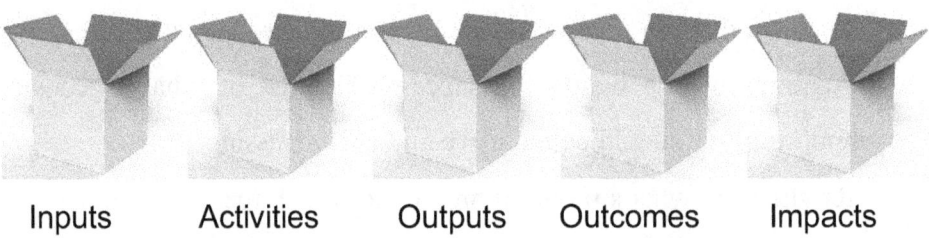

Inputs　　Activities　　Outputs　　Outcomes　　Impacts

You might be wondering where the goal went when we expanded to the inputs, activities, outputs, outcomes, and impacts concept. Because everything you are planning, everything you are doing is towards the goal, think of it this way:

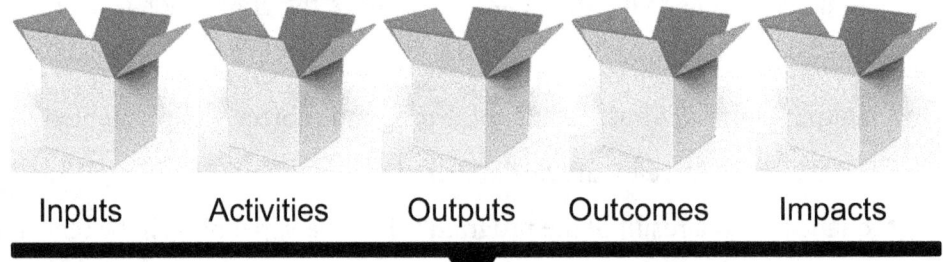

Inputs　　Activities　　Outputs　　Outcomes　　Impacts

Goal/Mission

This exercise can be completed with a variety of platforms:
- Boxes and notes in the center of a table
- Sticky notes on the wall or a whiteboard
- Virtual/online visual collaboration or planning board

We use these inputs (resources) for these activities (actions or endeavors) to produce these outputs (results) so that the stakeholders can experience these outcomes (change in these ways), leading to these impacts (long-term or permanent positive effects). Each *these* will be a list of its relevant program/project details.

Inputs	Activities	Outputs	Outcomes	Impacts
We use these inputs (resources)	for these activities or endeavors	to produce these (quantified) changes	so that the stakeholders can change in these ways	leading to these long-term positive effects

From the sample program Flip It Reverse Job and Career Fair, a sampling of inputs is identified as:

- Job Seekers with disabilities who want to be working
- Program staff
- Volunteers
- Area employers
- Portable office equipment (laptops and printers) and related supplies (ink and copy paper) for Resume Reboot and post-interview workshops
- Display boards and related supplies (scissors, markers, glue, tape) for the Display Board Build workshop
- Video recording equipment (iPad, tripod, backdrop) for Tell Me About It for mock interview workshop
- Sample clothing and full-length mirror for the Dress for Success workshop
- Transportation stipends and bus passes
- The DisAbility A-Plan: Employee of the Month Every Month handbooks for employers and hiring managers, job-seeking participants, and volunteers
- Venues for workshops and fair
- Healthy snacks and bottled water

Those inputs are required to make the following sampling of activities happen:

- Resume Reboot workshop
- Tell Me About It workshop
- Display Board Build workshop
- Dress for Success workshop
- Post-job fair wrap-up workshop
- Employers' Forum

- Flip It Reverse Job and Career Fair

They anticipate that from the activities, this sampling of outputs will be realized:

- 35 job seekers with disabilities will benefit from the Resume Reboot workshop
- 20 job seekers with disabilities will increase confidence through the Tell Me About It mock interview workshop
- 15 job seekers with disabilities will enhance the job search process with a display board highlighting their work experience, hobbies, and achievements
- 15 job seekers with disabilities will increase self-esteem from the Dress for Success workshop
- 25 job seekers will gain professional skills from the post-interview workshop
- 60 area businesses and hiring managers will be more familiar with the return on investment of hiring people with disabilities

From the outputs, these possible outcomes for job seekers can be tracked:

- Increased confidence
- Improved self-esteem
- Enriched communication skills
- Offer(s) of integrated, permanent, living-wage employment
- Increased client satisfaction through the improved likelihood of securing integrated, living-wage employment

From the outputs, these possible outcomes for employers and hiring managers can be tracked:

- Increased knowledge of accommodations for employees with disabilities
- Strengthened confidence in creating an inclusive culture in their workplace

These anticipated, trackable outcomes should affect this sampling of intended impacts:

- Reduced unemployment rate of people with disabilities who want to be working
- Increased self-sufficiency for employees with disabilities, reducing reliance on public assistance programs such as SNAP and Medicaid

- Enhanced life enjoyment for employees with disabilities
- Reduced turnover rates for employers, increasing profits for their businesses

We are about halfway there! Keep breathing!

THE PRESENTATION –

It would be somewhat awkward to send five boxes with scraps of paper in each to the grantmaker. So we need to convert THE TOOL to THE PRESENTATION. Whether the tool is used for planning or to strengthen a grant proposal, a logic model replaces lengthy narratives with a bullet-like list of succinctly worded descriptors that are presented in a diagram or table which illustrates the logical relationship among key program/project elements (inputs, activities, and outputs). Traditional (logic model) diagrams can be as uncomplicated as a table with three columns and as many rows as needed or as complex as schemes of boxes of jargon and buzzwords with arrows pointing in several directions that often backtrack or skip, or something in between.

Creating the presentation does not require a high-level skill set in infographics, Excel, or Powerpoint. However, it is expected that a logic model follows a format of bordered content. Here are a few examples of logic model presentational formats. All are acceptable; most are not necessary or recommended for typical nonprofit planning or grant proposals.

GOAL	OBJECTIVES	OUTCOMES

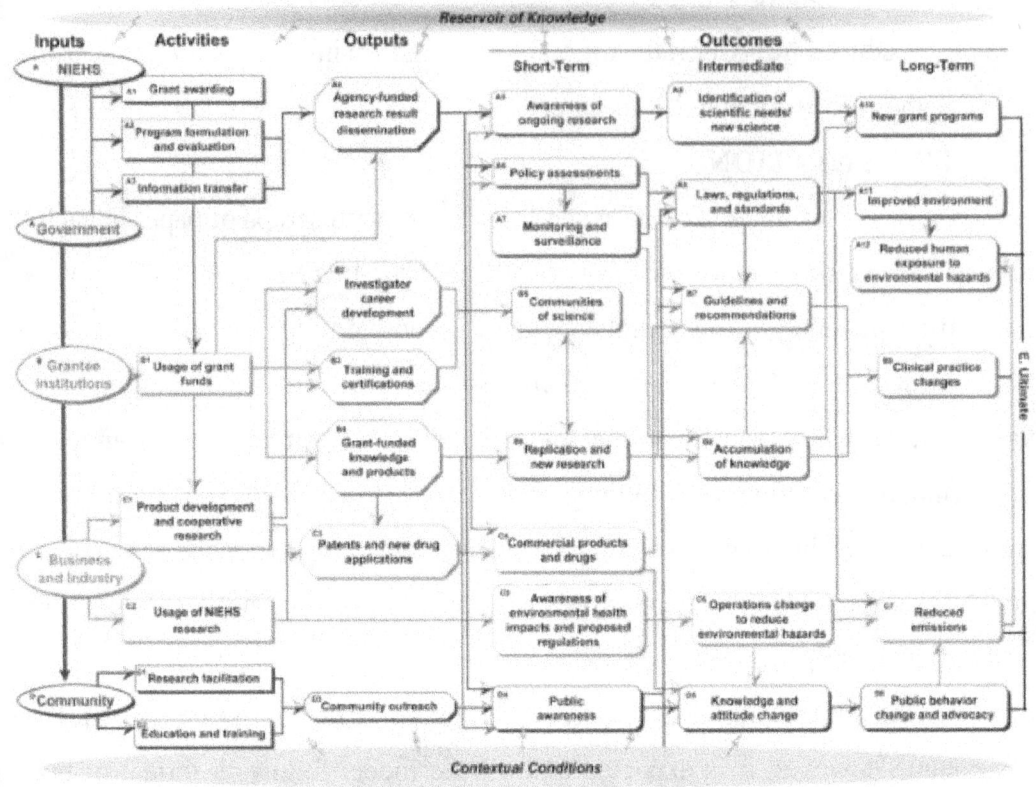

As you can see, there is more than one iteration of a logic model. While there are many, they all have one thing in common—they are a graphic depiction of a project/program plan. This is our logic model format:

Inputs	Activities	Outputs	Outcomes	Impacts

The most common presentation for a grant proposal is a table with five columns and as many rows as necessary. Programs/projects and funding gaps with multiple inputs, activities, and outputs are best presented with models that are larger than the common three-column version illustrated with Goal, Objectives, and Outcomes as headers. The five-column version appears more complicated than a simple three-column table. (Please note that I said, "appears more complicated." As you learn more about and become comfortable taking the components out of the boxes to enter them into the columns and rows, the task remains straightforward regardless of the number of components and details. Therefore, developing a logic model is not complicated!)

PUTTING IT ALL TOGETHER –

Where to put what? Multiple inputs, activities, and outputs often have some crossover. This is the appearance of complexity that was mentioned earlier. For example, one input might benefit more than one activity. Similarly, more than one activity might contribute to multiple outputs. For presentation purposes, the input could be listed in three separate rows in a simple table to be represented adequately in the planning and the grant proposal. Notice that the narratives in the second column of the row in the logic model below are the same phrases that completed the explanation at the end of the previous section, THE TOOL. (Please note that the descriptions in the second row of the above logic model will be removed from your final model; they have been added below to fully explain the logic model process.) You will not describe what each column title means to the funder. The brief descriptions are included only to clarify how to accurately identify which of the five elements is appropriate for each detail.

Inputs	Activities	Outputs	Outcomes	Impacts
We use these inputs (resources)	for these activities or endeavors	to produce these (quantified) changes	so that the stakeholders can change in these ways	leading to these long-term positive effects

The content for each column and row in the logic model is in the boxes. Each piece of paper in each 'cardboard' box (from THE TOOL section) represents the logic model's content and has its distinct entry in the logic model. Each input, activity, and outcome is added to the table systematically. A program or funding gap may have many components and details. Sometimes, the more money being sought translates to more components and details. Programs and projects can be multi-pronged, which again can result in multiple and interactive components and details. Be sure to include every component and detail—duplicated, irrelevant (to a specific grant but not the program), and inconsequential points can be deleted during final edits. Be aware that formatting, spacing, number of pages, or word/character limitations can affect how much content will make the final draft of a grant proposal.

Inputs	Activities	Outputs	Outcomes	Impacts
We use these inputs (resources)	*for these activities or endeavors*	*to produce these (quantified) changes*	*so that the stakeholders can change in these ways*	*leading to these long-term positive effects*
Job seekers with disabilities who want to be working	Resume Reboot workshop	35 job seekers will benefit from the Resume Reboot workshop	Increased confidence	Reduced unemployment rate of people with disabilities who want to be working
Program staff	Tell Me About It mock interview workshop		Improved self-esteem	
Volunteers		20 job seekers will increase confidence through the Tell Me About It mock interview workshop	Enriched communication skills	Increased self-sufficiency for employees with disabilities, reducing reliance on public assistance programs
Area employers	Display Board Build workshop			
Portable office equipment for Resume Reboot workshop and post-job fair wrap-up	Dress for Success workshop		Offer(s) of integrated, permanent, living-wage employment	
	Flip Reverse Job and Career Fair	60 area businesses will be more familiar with the ROI of disability inclusion		
Display boards and related supplies for Display Board Build workshop				

The essential details required to implement the program to completion, including impact, are listed. It is time to make the logical connections for the entire program/project to tell the whole story of how the program realizes a strong impact. Notice that the explanation for each column (We use these inputs (resources) for these activities or endeavors to produce these quantified changes so that the stakeholders can change in these ways leading to these long-term positive effects) is eliminated on the final logic model on the next page.

Inputs	Activities	Outputs	Outcomes	Impacts
Job seekers with disabilities who want to be working	Resume Reboot workshop	35 job seekers will benefit from the Resume Reboot workshop	Increased confidence	Reduced unemployment rate of people with disabilities who want to be working
Program staff	Tell Me About It mock interview workshop	20 job seekers will increase confidence through the Tell Me About It mock interview workshop	Improved self-esteem	
Volunteers			Enriched communication skills	Increased self-sufficiency for employees with disabilities, reducing reliance on public assistance programs
Area employers	Display Board Build workshop			
Portable office equipment for Resume Reboot workshop and post-job fair wrap-up	Dress for Success workshop		Offer(s) of integrated, permanent, living-wage employment	
	Flip Reverse Job and Career Fair	60 area businesses will be more familiar with the ROI of disability inclusion	Increased employer knowledge of accommodations for employees with disabilities	Enhanced life enjoyment for employees with disabilities
Display boards and related supplies for Display Board Build workshop	Post-job fair wrap-up workshop			
	Employers' Forum	15 job seekers will enhance the job search process with a display board highlighting their work experience, achievements, and hobbies	Strengthened employer confidence in creating an inclusive culture in their workplace	Reduced turnover rates for employers, increasing profits for their businesses
Video recording equipment for Tell Me About It mock interview workshop				
Sample clothing and full-length mirror for Dress for Success workshop		60 area hiring managers and businesses will be more familiar with the return on investment of hiring people with disabilities		
Transportation stipends and bus passes				

Congratulations! You survived completing your logic model! Big exhale!

Now that you have a logic model, what can you do with it? Logic models can play an undeniable role in strengthening grant proposals. We have determined that and demonstrated that. You also need to identify other information resources for which logic models can be used and vice versa. For example, anticipated outputs, outcomes, and impacts can be, in part, determined from data and metrics collected while researching support for the Needs Assessment and Needs Statement or in the development of the Program/Project Description or Executive Summary. Data and metrics might also be moored in materials of evidence-based programs/projects explored during earlier planning. Logic models are where metrics and data meet program/project descriptions.

The logic model is also expedient for linking the logical process from the assumptions about the outputs to the outcomes and, subsequently, from the outcomes to the impacts in program/project development and evaluations. Using evidence-based program/project strategies will help make these assumptions more accurate. When developed thoroughly, all possible outcomes are inventoried in the logic model. It will show what to measure and determine how to measure each outcome by brainstorming during the planning process. A logic model provides a summary of outcomes available to measure for evaluating the program/project (i.e., what to measure).

The logic model is functional for outcomes evaluation, as well. (There is a difference between what outcomes are available to measure and what outcomes to measure for evaluative purposes. They are not the same thing.) The outcomes evaluation makes it possible to anticipate the impacts. As reviewed in the block on "Evaluations," some outcomes will have a single quantifiable aspect (i.e., evaluation). Others will have multiple ways to assess benchmarks. Depending upon what information is rooted in the assessments, the strength of links between outcomes and impacts, or lack thereof, can be established. If the links are weak from an output to an outcome(s), that specific outcome might not need to be evaluated at all; that outcome can still be included in the logic model. Remember:

Inputs and activities make up your planned work;

the outputs, outcomes, and impacts represent your intended results.

The logic model is invaluable in setting the framework of what to measure for evaluations. (The decision of how to measure the outcomes is discussed in the block on "Evaluations.")

Additionally, budgets and logic models can be best friends. The budget is closely linked to the logic model because everything required to implement the program/project must be represented in the budget and should be represented in the logic model. Budgets are data, hard data. The budget data is an integral part of the overall program/project. The logic model is a great tool to cross-reference with the budget to ensure every part and piece of the program/project has budget allocations. If a comparison of various parts and components of the grant proposal, including the completed logic model, is made, some repetition of information is revealed. That is common and to be expected. It also demonstrates that the organization or program/project manager is well-organized, well-prepared, and knows how to effectively communicate the processes to achieve the program/project target—a target or mission that is ultimately attained by impact!

The link between the list of inputs and the program/project budget should be obvious. The inputs do not list a dollar amount on the logic model, but the corresponding budget entries do. The correlation is clear, though, because the budget narrative will clarify how a line-item total was determined. When the budget, budget narrative, and logic model are compared, a grant proposal reviewer will unmistakably see that all possible expenditures have been accounted for to complete the program/project for which funding is being applied.

Additionally, it is evident by the logic model that all funds are allocated for the most prudent use of the funder's money. The budget, budget narrative, and logic model mirror one another but are differentiated in style and format. Each format conveys the information in a requested or particular way, demonstrating comprehensive planning, sustainability, and efficient use of resources to address the need.

The table below does not show comprehensive planning, sustainability, and efficient use of resources to address the need. This type of table is often confused with a logic model. It could be used in nonprofit planning and grant proposals, but not as a logic model because there are no outcomes, and a purpose is not the same as an impact. And, of course, there are no logical connections.

MIWD Partnerships
Fiscal Year 20**

Partner	Product, Service	Result	Purpose
Disability Advocates of Central Ohio	Referrals; partner for community events	Additional support for people with disabilities who want to be working	Increased job seeker participants
Happy Carrot Catering	Caterer	Healthy snacks, bottled water	In-kind donation
Trucks 'r Us	Vans and drivers who are licensed to transport people with disabilities	Transfer equipment and supplies between office and venues; transportation for job seekers with disabilities	Help offset transportation costs

A few miscellaneous thoughts about logic models:

- Do not try to pass off a columned table as a logic model. A table is appropriate for showing partnerships and collaborations. However, a table is not the same as a well-thought-out logic model. A table can still serve as a graphic, but it has a very different purpose than a logic model because a table does not illustrate the logical connections.

- For the highest efficiency, complete a logic model for each program/project and funding necessity before starting a grant proposal. The best time to develop logic models is immediately after the following year's budget is approved. That way, they are done for the year and are ready to add to any grant proposal. Remember, any document or element for a grant proposal can be edited and updated to accommodate changes; having that master version completed will save time, stress, and money over the long run. Architects design before they build; grant proposal writers are architects and can create a blueprint before beginning the writing process.

- On the internet, logic model samples show short-term and medium-range outcomes in a seven-columned model. This is cumbersome for grant proposals. They are great for checking and evaluating the progress of benchmarks of programs but not so much as a visual presentation. (Some federal grant applications require short-, medium-, and long-range benchmarks. Follow the same process to complete the additional two columns.)
- A logic model also breaks copy content for easier reading in a grant proposal. Presenting a logic model in a grant proposal allows for white space and an alternative style of content that can add interest and reduce the monotony of reading for the grant reviewer. A logic model also adds credibility and a polished touch to grant proposals.
- As always, thoroughly check spelling and other mechanical consistencies such as spacing, punctuation, font, and type size in each box. Do not solely rely on spelling and grammar check features in the word processing software.
- Remember, a logic model represents intention, not reality. A logic model focuses on expected outcomes.
- Remember, a logic model does not address, "Are we doing the right thing?"
- Everything you put into a logic model can help you write a grant proposal.

Just remember to breathe, and that:

Inputs and activities make up your planned work;

outputs, outcomes, and impacts represent your intended results.

"The process of developing the model is an opportunity to chart the course. It is a conscious process that creates an explicit understanding of the challenges ahead, the resources available, and the timetable in which to hit the target." (W.K. Kellogg Foundation)

Tarra Nystrom

Data and Metrics for Grant Proposals

You do not have to know or even understand algorithms, statistics, or computer science to work with data and metrics. You do not have to be a data scientist to analyze data of actionable insights for inclusion in grant funding requests. It is beneficial if you have experience with hypothesis, randomization, or sampling, but most of us do not. For grant applications, you have to know what data and metrics to find and how to use them; you do not have to be a research analyst. You do not have to conduct your own research, either. However, evaluating programs and projects by listing inputs, activities, outputs, outcomes, and impacts is different from doing research. Program/project evaluation explanations are required in most grant applications, and reporting is a mandatory part of the grant process. (Program/project evaluation is covered in detail in that block.)

Data and metrics are second only to logic models for evoking fear in many of us working in nonprofits or applying for grants. Breaking data and metrics into easy-to-understand parts will eliminate that fear. Data are the facts and statistics collected together for reference or analysis; the things known or assumed as facts founding the basis of reasoning or calculation. Next, metrics are methods of measuring something or the results obtained from this—a system or standard of measurement. For grant proposal writing purposes, metrics can be further defined as standards of measurement by which efficiency, performance, progress, or quality of a plan, process, program, project, or product can be assessed.

Data are collected to use in the metrics. Data are irrelevant without their metrics.

Know What to Collect –

So, what data is needed for the metrics for the grant proposal to win the funding? Chances are you already know the basic answer to this question, and you do not realize it! We need numbers and narratives. We need hard data and soft data. Then, we can learn how to craft the data for the most considerable advantage in grant proposals.

The most persuasive grant proposals combine hard data and soft data to demonstrate:
- What the problem looks like in the targeted area
- Why the situation matters
- What is causing the need the program/project intends to address

Hard data are facts, figures, and research findings. Hard data are proof that the program is evidence-based. Hard data more convincingly attest to the need (Needs Statements and Assessment) than speak directly to the funder focus. Hard data sets up the soft data for optimal impact. Soft data are quotes, stories, and anecdotes. Soft data are narratives rooted in fact. Although soft data are qualitative, they must be quantified or verified in some way, not merely a casual opinion. These quotes, stories, and anecdotes should come from experts or targeted constituencies of the program/project's impacts. For grant proposals, soft data should closely correlate to the funder focus. Data and metrics support the evidence-based program design as well as the evaluation and reporting plans. Simply saying there is a need is not enough to compel grant funders to write a check. Data and metrics must support the need.

The following are examples suggesting how data can be used in grant applications. We will use unemployment for people with disabilities who want to be working as the exemplified funder focus. The suggestions are not a complete list but a variety to represent the possibilities. Note that "want to be working" is consistently referenced for our target constituency. In this specific (hypothetical) program, there is a discernibility between the ideas of people with disabilities, people with disabilities who are unemployed, and people with disabilities who are unemployed but want to be working.

- ✓ For the situation causing concern (the "what"), use facts, figures, and research findings (hard data) to show the number of people with disabilities who are unemployed but want to be working, to compare the unemployment rate for people with no disabilities and those with disabilities who want to be working, to show the demographics of the target group, or to highlight how unemployment among individuals with disabilities who want to be working in the target area compares to the same group in another area. There is no need for soft data to support the situation. The facts and figures suffice; save the "heart-string tugging" quotes, stories, and anecdotes (soft data) for the "why" of the problem and "how" to positively impact the problem.

- ✓ For the significance of the situation ("why" it matters), use facts, figures, and research findings (hard data) to define the problems caused by or related to unemployment for individuals with disabilities who want to be working. This data set could include increases in poverty levels, increases in reliance on public benefits (SNAP, Medicaid, etc.), stress- and nutrition-related health issues, decreased independence, and diminished self-esteem. Use quotes, stories, or anecdotes (soft data) to humanize the effects of unemployment on people with disabilities who want to be working, amplifying the diminished stakeholder group's voice or challenged lives.

- ✓ The cause of the problem might be a "when" or "who" or "where" or "how," or a combination of any of these factors. There might be more than one of any or all of these factors causing the problem. For the cause of the problem, use facts, figures, and research findings (hard data) to quantify, for example, employer limitations such as lack of knowledge about accommodations or training, unfamiliarity with employment programs or resources for hiring people with disabilities, or need for information about skill and educational levels of job seekers with disabilities. Hard data can highlight the causes of unemployment for job seekers with disabilities, such as quantifying access to or availability of job development programs or vocational on-the-job mentoring. Stories, testimonials, and anecdotes (soft data) can increase impact and emphasize the advantage of grant funding by presenting the perspective of the appropriate stakeholder group(s), such as the job seekers with disabilities who want to be working or employers needing more help with hiring people with disabilities.

Figuring out what to measure or track—the sources of data—is as simple as knowing what directs the mission. The mission is achieved with inputs being used for planned activities producing outputs and outcomes, resulting in intended impacts. These are the who, what, when, where, and how of the program/project or other organizational funding requirement.

- Who are the stakeholder group(s)?
- What outcomes and impact(s) are intended?
- What must be implemented (activities and outputs) to make the outcomes happen?
- When or in what timeframe must the outputs, outcomes, and impacts occur?
- What is the defined funding period? (This is different from the timeframe in which the program/project will be implemented.)
- Where do the activities take place?
- How are the inputs obtained?

Before collecting data, it is important to clarify what information you hope your data will reveal and how it will be used. This data should be both qualitative and quantitative. The best way to do this is to identify specific questions (Steering Queries) about the program/project that will guide you throughout the data collection process. To help determine what the Steering Queries should be, turn to the organization's strategic plan. If there is no formal strategic plan, the same information can be found in a combination of places such as the program/project description, budget and budget narrative, job descriptions, evaluation methods or plans, partnership and collaboration agreements, noted from strategy conversations of board meetings, or a logic model. The strategic plan (or other sources of program/project details) expresses the impact (the anticipated changes that will improve upon the need in the community) and outlines how the impact will be accomplished (the inputs and activities deemed necessary for the expected outputs and outcomes). The Steering Queries for the data collection can be developed with something as simple as brainstorming about the anticipated and hoped-for impact(s). Here is what I mean:

Impact: Assist unemployed individuals with disabilities who want to be working procure living-wage employment for increased self-reliance and independence, decreased dependence on public assistance, and enhanced lifestyle.

Strategy: These inputs (required human, financial, and physical resources; tangible and intangible resources) will be used to implement these activities (Flip It Reverse Job and Career Fair, et al.) to produce the outputs (quantified results) for these outcomes (so that stakeholders can change in these ways) leading to these impacts (improved-upon need in community).

Steering Queries: How many job seekers with disabilities who want to be working participated in the reverse job and career fair? How many job seekers with disabilities who want to be working participated in each of the Resume Reboot, Tell Me About It, Dress for Success, and Display Board Build pre-job fair activities? Did the pre-job fair activities' participants find value in the activities? How many job seekers with disabilities who want to be working used transportation vouchers or stipends for the reverse job and career fair, pre-job fair activities, and post-job fair activities? How many employers attended the reverse job and career fair? How many employers participated in the Employers' Forum? Did the employers who participated in the Employers' Forum find value in the information? How many total volunteer hours were used for the Flip It Reverse Job and Career Fair and related activities? How many social media messages were posted for Flip It Reverse Job and Career Fair? How many responses to social media messages were recorded for Flip It Reverse Job and Career Fair? This is a sampling of Steering Queries, not an exhaustive list.

Steering Queries are part of knowing what to collect; items for questionnaires, surveys, polls, and open-ended responses are part of collecting. Remember, the Steering Queries will address what has to be measured, which could be one component of the program/project or every program component. Additionally, the Steering Queries are not the same as the questions asked in questionnaires, surveys, polls, or open-ended responses. To emphasize: Steering Queries are part of knowing what to collect; items for questionnaires, surveys, polls, and open-ended responses are part of collecting (covered later in this block).

Figuring out what to measure (or track) is much easier when there are those Steering Queries because they narrow the focus. You can be more focused when you work

SMARTer. By identifying the specific, measurable, achievable, relevant, and time-bound parts of the program/project, energies can be directed to a finite and manageable set of data that can be calculated or analyzed. This is an excellent place to point out that the data and metrics compiled for the overall organization might differ from those examined for a particular program/project and used in a grant proposal, depending upon the size and scope of your organization. Remember that metrics can be further defined as standards of measurement by which efficiency, performance, progress, or quality of a plan, process, program, project, or product can be assessed for grant proposal writing purposes. A correlation can be made between efficiency, performance, or progress and the overall aspiration of working SMARTer. And starting at the program/project level makes learning and mastering data and metrics much more manageable.

It is easy to want to track everything; that is why there is the step of developing Steering Queries. Never track or collect data for the sake of tracking or collecting. It is a waste of valuable time and can reduce efficiency. Sometimes, tracking everything can confuse the data analysis crucial to a grant application. Another threat to efficiency is that tracking everything can delay analysis, rendering the data no longer relevant. Using collected data relevant to a specific grant funding request ensures consistent and expedited reports. Also, recognize that what is appropriate for one grant proposal might not be so for another; the relevance addresses the funding gap to be filled. Likewise, what is relevant to collect for one program/project might not fit another, or what another organization tracks for a similar program/project might not be appropriate for your purposes.

Once you know what Steering Queries should be answered, you need to set the purpose of collecting and analyzing your data. The purpose of a particular collection and analysis is the message or point you want to emphasize with the facts and figures. Honing in on a specific purpose is important because not only will it help determine what data is collected (i.e., from the Steering Queries) but also how it is collected, analyzed, and the results made meaningful in supporting the expected impacts. The purpose of using the data and metrics for grant proposals should concentrate on the funder's guidelines and focus and the specific funding request areas (the funding gaps to be filled) of the program/project or another funding gap.

For the case of general operating, technology, volunteer-oriented, capacity-building, or other non-program/project grant funding requests and for-profit or arts-related endeavors, the data and metrics should emphasize organizational or non-program/project strategies and impacts. The Steering Queries will likely indicate the type of grant funding necessary to realize the impacts around which data is collected and influence how the collected data is used.

Another consideration of data collection is what type of data to amass. You might choose to collect quantitative data or qualitative data, or both. Quantitative data are measures of values or counts and are expressed as numbers. This type of data is in the form of counts or numbers, where each data set has a unique numerical value. Quantitative data are data about numeric variables (i.e., how many, how much, how often) to understand quantities or frequency, determine cause-and-effect, make comparisons, or establish numerical baselines.

Alternately, qualitative data is defined as the data that approximates and characterizes. Qualitative data can be observed and recorded. This data type is non-numerical and provides essential context to help turn the data into a story. In fact, during the early stages of a program/project, qualitative data may be all that is available to collect. Quantitative data can be obtained for qualitative data such as opinions and attitudes, multiple perspectives, and to identify approximate (rather than exact) information. For example, the total number of participants who feel the Tell Me About It activity was more beneficial than the other pre- and post-job and career fair activities can be tracked. Additionally, the reason(s) why each participant found that particular activity was most beneficial can also be tracked and reported. A best practice is to collect qualitative data whenever possible, as it is almost always possible to collect quantitative data.

It is helpful to know that both quantitative and qualitative data can come from internal or external sources. Internal sources of data are collected from within the organization and close partners. External sources of data collection, analysis, and evaluation are collected from others' research outside the organization. Internal and external sources are also referred to as primary and secondary sources of data. Like internal sources, primary sources provide raw information and first-hand evidence, giving direct access to the subject of the research. Analogous to external sources, secondary information imparts second-hand information from others not directly associated with the program/project or organization.

Once you understand your Steering Queries, the purpose of collecting data, and the type of data to be collected, the next step is to define what requires measuring to answer the Steering Queries. Data and metrics are how results are measured. Even though a grant funding request is for a program/project or other gaps in organizational funding with unknown but expected results, it is crucial to anticipate or predict the intended outcomes and impacts as accurately as possible. Predictions often are developed through data collection and analysis of others' research. And, of course, when reporting as part of the grant funding agreement, it is crucial to have tracked accurate participation levels, benchmarks, and more. Your Steering Queries, on occasion, might lead to modifying existing measures or creating new ones altogether. Steering Queries, remember, are derived from outputs, outcomes, and impacts that can lead to the revelation of new deliverables or previously unnoticed qualitative and quantitative measures to track. Defining what should be measured based on the Steering Queries is vital. Outputs can be defined by actual numbers that can be counted. Outcomes and impacts can be defined by answering what exact change is being sought and identifying various measures that prove the change occurred.

In the broad scheme of things, measurements are tied to outcomes. Outputs are required to realize outcomes. Outputs are how the outcomes and impacts are accomplished, and outcomes are the why. Remember:

- ✓ Outputs are the direct results of the program/project's implemented activities. These are concrete, quantifiable indicators of productivity. What can be quantified in the program/project? How many people will be reached? How many will participate? What events will occur, and how many?
- ✓ Outcomes are the short-term and intermediate benchmarks for the target constituency during and after program/project activities. These are the

program's short-term benefits, as opposed to the long-range, big-picture changes you expect to see. Outcomes should be quantified whenever possible.

✓ Outputs are the investment, and outcomes are the ROI (return on investment). Outputs on their own do not prove anyone or anything is better off. Data and metrics help translate the outputs to value and show that the targeted constituents are better off.

For grant proposal writing purposes, choose the outcomes that best align with the funder's desired outcomes—their focus. Here are a few examples to get you started:

- Increased knowledge and learning
- Changed attitudes
- Increased readiness
- Reduction or elimination of undesirable behavior
- Increase in desirable behavior
- Maintenance of new behavior
- Increased social status
- Improved economic conditions
- Improved health conditions
- Increased economic development

Defining what should be measured involves being careful with the semantics used when composing the Steering Queries. Semantics count when counting! Here are a couple of considerations: Are you interested in an increase, decrease, or simply a change? Do you need to measure one indicator or multiple indicators to know if you are achieving your targets? Do your measurements reflect those implied by your Steering Queries? Are there other external factors not mentioned in program/project descriptions or other narratives to consider to interpret your measures accurately? Merely stating how many job seekers with disabilities participated in the Flip It Reverse Job and Career Fair is not sufficient or responsible.

Further, distinguishing between people with disabilities, people with disabilities who are unemployed, and people with disabilities who are unemployed but want to be working is an ideal illustration of how semantics can play into collection and analysis. Similarly, stating that 491 volunteer hours will be or were used by your nonprofit is minimal use of the measure for persuasive rhetoric in grant proposals. Quantifying that 491 volunteer hours are valued at $13,355.20 in FY 2019 (491 X $27.20 per hour value of each volunteer hour in 2019 as reported by IndependentSector.org) or that volunteers provided the equivalent of one part-time program assistant for one year makes the data relevant and useful. (This data was analyzed from external or secondary research by IndependentSector.com for the value of a volunteer hour in the nonprofit sector in the U.S., then comparing it to internal or primary data that a program assistant earns $12.00 per hour and works 20 per each of 52 weeks of a year.) As you can see, program/project metrics are not the only information that might be communicated in a grant proposal.

Beyond program/project impacts, you have the opportunity to demonstrate sustainability, social media and marketing reach, fundraising or operational efficiencies, partnership and collaboration benefits, or strength of the volunteer program, to suggest a few. For example, suppose the nonprofit industry rate of opened emails is 18.2%, and your open rate is 26.5%. In that case, this is a metric to be touted in particular content areas of a grant application.

Another example: Brag if the nonprofit's Operating Reliance Ratio (ORR) is above the industry standard of 80% efficiency. This metric is calculated from data collected about unrestricted program revenue divided by total expenses. ORR is an indicator of financial sustainability. Other ratios that elevate a grant application include the Fundraising Efficiency Ratio (FER). The FER, or how much money is spent to raise funds, is calculated with data collected about the unrestricted fundraising expenses divided by the unrestricted contributions. The Program/Project Efficiency Ratio (PER), an indicator of efficient money management in programming, is calculated from data collected about unrestricted program/project expenses divided by total expenses.

Unrestricted program revenue / total expenses = ORR
Unrestricted fundraising expenses / total unrestricted contribution = FER
Unrestricted program/project expenses / total expenses = PER

A very effective way to incorporate these ratios in a grant funding request is to include the numbers/ratios in a narrative that transitions. Rather than overtly stating, "MIWD's Operating Reliance Ratio is 83.4%," try something similar to, "By achieving a Program Efficiency Ratio of 83.4% in FY 2019, MIWD was able to leverage four additional sponsorships and an additional $895.00 in-kind donations for the Flip It Reverse Job and Career Fair."

Human resources adeptness is an oft-overlooked metric useful for some grant proposals. Human resource metrics are measurements used to determine the value and effectiveness of personnel initiatives, characteristically including turnover and time to hire, training, return on human capital, costs of labor, billable hours, and expenses per employee. Data collected on these can support sustainability, the likelihood of program/project growth, or credibility in the community, for example.

The Cost Per Unit of Service (CPUS) shows similar data to the Program/Project Efficiency Ratio. The CPUS describes this efficiency in terms of dollars rather than a percentage. It is still data. The Cost Per Unit of Service for a particular program or project is calculated by dividing the total program budget by the number of (actual) participants:

Total Budget / Total Participants = Cost per Unit of Service

$$\$17,833 / 96 = \$185.76$$

For budgeting, the expected number of participants is the only number available for calculation. Using the actual number of participants in reporting rather than the expected number increases the cost per unit. This reality cannot be avoided. Few programs/projects achieve 100% forecasted participation, and accurate reporting will show an increased CPUS.

The CPUS and benefit of costs related to them are persuasive metrics in grant proposals and complement the Cost Per Unit of Service data. A cost revenue analysis can reveal, for example, that a one-time investment of $12,000 for software will streamline the job development process for job seekers with disabilities, reducing the Cost Per Unit of Service from $185.76 to $115.35. The potential funder understands that the organization will use all donor dollars more efficiently. This benefit can be communicated in budget narratives and Program/Project Descriptions and Evaluations. Consider cost revenue analysis as:

CPUS + Impact = Cost Benefit

Even when the components and process of measurements are understood, data and metrics can evoke fear and dread. They are associated with science, and most of us do not have scientific prowess, especially when we work in nonprofits—social services, advocacy, rescue, or public policy creation. It is easy to avoid the task that we fear or dread. It is easy to feel that we are not executing measurements competently or will not execute flawlessly. Fear not. Even with data and metrics, imperfection does not become refutable. Because most nonprofits do not have the money to hire professional research firms, the value of internal capacity for research and familiarity with reliable, external sources becomes vital. There is value even in imperfection, believe it or not. In terms of data and metrics, imperfection does not mean wrong, without value, or unjustified. Imperfect data and metrics refer to anecdotal, interpretive, subjective, or qualitative, or that which relies on a small sample, uncontrolled situational factors, or cannot be precisely replicated. And that is okay. When submitting a proposal for grant funding, we are not inventing the next dynamic prescriptive medicine or advanced space-age technology. (Okay, most of us aren't!) The predicted outcomes and impacts are reliable because the program/project is evidence-based, the need is supported by research and fact, the budget is comprehensive, the staff is qualified and well-trained, and the evaluation methods are reasonable and responsible. It is better to have imperfect data and metrics than to have none at all. Reasonably relevant imperfection can establish helpful and trustworthy information.

Hopefully, the idea of useful imperfection has diminished most of the dread of data and metrics. The dread is replaced with the balance of what can be and what should be measured within the organization's capacity. It goes back to, "Do not track for the sake of tracking." Just because you can count it or ask an open-ended question about it does not mean it addresses any of the Steering Queries. What if something cannot be counted, but the analysis is necessary to assess success? The seemingly intangible requires being measured, but how? Because mission statements are inherently vague and impacts more often are written in broad-reaching terms, almost conceptual, than with precise standards, how can vagueness or concept be measured rather than merely explained? Perceptions garnered from stakeholders can be anecdotal, interpretive, subjective, or qualitative. Even if the analysis is based on the data collector's experiences, it will reflect the stakeholder's viewpoint. The analysis is quite imperfect, as set by the traditional scientific process, but quite beneficial to the examination and evaluation of the data. Therefore, it is advantageous to the scrutiny of how close to expected the impacts were achieved.

Here are some suggestions of what to collect: Specific program/project and other organization-specific funding needs will expand this list:

- Demographics (age, race, gender, etc.)
- Services delivered
- Specific, identified outcomes
- Media/press mentions
- Social media metrics (views, followers)
- Communication metrics (opens, click-throughs)
- Social enterprise metrics (sales, revenue, customer demographics)
- Participation levels
- Participant and stakeholder feedback
- Attention metrics
- Volunteer hours
- Volunteer demographics
- In-kind donation categories and levels
- Costs and revenues (ORR, FER, PER, CPUS)

Ready to Collect –

For the execution of the grant proposal, the Steering Queries provide direction for what data should be gathered. You know the types of sources from which data will be collected. The purpose(s) of the data is demarcated for various parts of the proposal. You are ready to collect! The collection process involves identifying resources for the data collection process, creating a data collection plan, and deciding the best method(s).

Identifying resources to collect the data (for grant proposals) requires assessing the grant proposal writer and their team's capacity. Capacity is the ability to do something. People do data collection with tools such as Excel, Word, or other software. Having adequate capacity is having enough people with the right tools and experience to use those tools. Does the grant proposal writer or team have the capacity to collect data in SMART ways? Analyze the SMART Grant Proposal Writer/Team Capacity for Data and Metrics:

Specific—Created Steering Queries (inputs, outputs)

Measurable—Understand and execute Steering Queries (outcomes, impacts)

Achievable—Expertise (knowing or understanding the program/project or need in the community to collect the data that competently reflect the intended outcomes and impacts) and facilitation skills for collecting (ability to create questionnaires, surveys, or categories from which to count)

Relevant—Develop data-minded storytelling skills (the ability to compel action and evoke emotion in the grant reviewer from the available facts, figures, and stories)

Time-bound—Allow enough time to collect data to prepare and submit a grant proposal

If the current grant proposal writer/team and tools are not at the necessary capacity, resources (people and tools) can be added to the team. Some suggested capacity-building team resources include organizational governance (board of directors), program/project staff, experienced and knowledgeable volunteers, development staff, accounting team, corporate and small business funders, private donors, program/project participants, collaborators, and in-kind partners. The potential internal resources can write better and more accurate contributions for grant proposals. The partners and participants rely on outcomes, while donors and funders see impacts, recognize sustainability, and feel a part of the mission—all increasing engagement.

Creating a collection plan involves outlining personnel, timeframes, methods, and budget items specific to the data collection not already included in program/project costs and other activities necessary to address the Steering Queries. Because every grant application is different, the data and metrics presentation might never look the same way twice. However, be assured that you will not start from scratch every time a new grant application is started. The collection plan gives a streamlined approach for each data-gathering endeavor. Resources and methods probably are least familiar concerning data and metrics because the other parts of the collection plan are used in most other reasons for planning in the nonprofit world.

Because most grant proposal writers are not data scientists, having reliable, go-to data and research sources are paramount. Some of these reliable, go-to sources are no-brainers, some are learned, and some are accidentally discovered. The internet can be the grant proposal writer's best friend or worst foe when it comes to reliable, go-to sources. That is why "reliable" is so crucial. As part of your collection plan, choose three to five go-to sources for each program/project or other organizational funding purposes for which you feel grant funding is likely. Additionally, seek out a couple of local experts to provide a linear perspective on the funding need and the community. By including a finite set of resources in the plan, much time is saved, a lesser sense of being overwhelmed is achieved, a solid message is created, and you quickly learn what trusted information resembles. This is not to say that you will never use other resources for your research. You will. You do not have the time or patience for the tens of thousands of results that pop up for one keyword search.

Additionally, the word or character count restrictions in some grant proposals do not allow for the vast amount of information available. Your go-to sources must categorically supply hard data and can provide soft data. Begin with the easy stuff: Information from the government. The U.S. Census Bureau and its Community Survey, Centers for Disease Control and Prevention, U.S. Bureau of Labor Statistics, U.S. Department of Housing and Urban Development, U.S. Department of Education, National Science Foundation, World Health Organization, United Nations, and the state and municipal equivalents are reliable and easily accessible. National associations for specific areas of study or interest/advocacy, respected and unbiased news reporting, academic and white papers, and community foundation studies are remarkable sources of go-to data that are current and relevant.

(A note about county-level reporting: Some county reporting can be skewed by the existence of "millionaire syndrome," depending upon the demographics. "Millionaire syndrome" not only relates to the pockets of extreme wealth or lack thereof but any data point existing in one extreme or another in a county. The "millionaire syndrome" is explained as a small pocket of extreme wealth in an otherwise average or below-average area. For example, a smaller community has homes valued multiple times higher than those of the rest of the homes in the county or household income levels significantly higher than throughout the rest of the county. The "millionaire syndrome" occurs when there are enough in this smaller community to change that averages noticeably. Be mindful of this possibility if pulling data from a vastly diverse area.)

The experts could be you or the program/project manager, an academic, a community leader, a business owner, or the mayor to provide a frame of reference. The experts ought to have full knowledge of the situation, be credible, and support the mission in some way. The local experts will offer more soft data than hard data but do not discount those in your community with valid, purposeful hard data to bolster the funding request.

There are many methods to collect data from the resources, including counting and tabulation via surveys, polls, questionnaires, observations, interviews, focus groups, and searching through other publicly available data. To determine which method is best, consider how you will obtain each of your data points. Based on your Steering Queries, what is the best way to discern the answers? The answers best analyzed with quantitative data usually seek statistical information using counting via surveys, polls, and questionnaires (with closed-ended questions). Yes/No is more easily counted than opinion or perspective. The answers best examined for qualitative data commonly consist of open-ended questions and explanatory answers with little or no numerical value. Qualitative data is an excellent way to acquire an awareness of a stakeholder group's thoughts and behavior (maybe the ones you identified using quantitative research but could not analyze in greater detail). Qualitative data collection methods can be used to:

- Discover new ideas
- Uncover alternative problems
- Ascertain additional opportunities
- Test value and accuracy
- Originate predictions

- Explore a particular data point in greater detail
- Explain the numbers obtained through quantitative gathering techniques

This data type is collected through observation methods, one-on-one interviews, conducting focus groups or case studies, and similar processes.

For purposes of the collection plan, it is worth noting that quantitative data typically requires less time to collect and analyze and is cheaper to facilitate than data for qualitative analysis. Also, note that qualitative data can be counted. An example of this is tabulating the number of similar anecdotal responses and grouping them as a range or in categories such as "strongly disliked" to "strongly liked."

Remember, questions asked in questionnaires, surveys, polls, or open-ended responses are not the same as the Steering Queries. The Steering Queries are part of knowing what to collect, and questions for questionnaires, surveys, polls, and open-ended responses are part of collecting. However, the questions asked in questionnaires, surveys, polls, or open-ended responses are rooted in the Steering Queries.

Now put your data and metrics to work by analyzing the information and drawing conclusions that answer the Steering Queries. This is the tactical portion of data and metrics. Each Steering Query might require its own type of analysis. The type of analysis is the tactic to be used when drawing conclusions. The analysis is about finding patterns in the gathered information or the lack of patterns. Facts, statistics, and trends (all part of a purposeful analytical framework) can illuminate patterns in the stakeholders' participation and perspectives, the levels and diversity of participation, changes resulting from their engagement, and much more. Patterns are revealed when raw data is transformed with a combination of arithmetic and detailed measurements. The facts, stats, and trends framework are explained in these terms:

- Facts—counts, sums, or numbers
- Statistics—fundamental descriptive indicators (mean, median, mode, distribution)
- Trends—looking at the data over time, seeking identifiable change expressed by percent change or percent difference; percent change/difference within the

same group at varying points in time or between groups at the same time or at different points in time.

Present the Data and Metrics –

Storytelling with data can inspire action by directing focus deliberately and eliminating clutter. Grant proposal reviewers discern rationale from what was tracked, collected, and recorded from easy-to-interpret visuals of the data and metrics. Like not needing to be a data scientist to use data and metrics in your grant proposals, you do not need to be a graphic artist or Excel expert to make compelling visual presentations from the data and metrics. We will break it into parts and steps that are easy to cognize and execute. Storytelling in grant proposals is more than heart-string tugging. Adding the ability to tell a story with data complements the narrative portions of the grant proposal. Data and metrics are used for clarification, persuasion, evaluation, and elevating the style.

Knowing the type of data (qualitative or quantitative) is most important when creating visuals for the data and metrics. Visualization is a part of the research (tracking and collecting) and analysis processes. If the information cannot be interpreted, it is worthless; visuals in a grant proposal are for knowledge sharing and clarification. The information is shared through tables, graphs, charts, plots, semantic networks, concept maps, and storyboarding. (Samples of each of these are found in the *SMART Money Grant Writing: SMART Charts Workbook*.) Data display can be the demise of a tremendous evaluative or analytic effort. Here is a guide on how to best display your data.

Quantitative and qualitative data visualization –

Quantitative data is used to compare values, show composition (individual parts of the whole), explain distribution (understand outliers, norms, and range), analyze trends (changes or differences over time), and understand the relationships between data sets.

Comparing values is best displayed in these visuals: Column, bar, line, circular area, scatter plot, and bullet graphs.

Composition is best displayed in these visuals: Stacked bar, pie, stacked column, area, and waterfall graphs.

Distribution is best displayed in these visuals: Column, bar, line, and scatter plot graphs.

Trends are best displayed in these visuals: Column, line, and dual-axis graphs. Relationships between data sets are best displayed in these visuals: Line, scatter plot, and bubble graphs.

Qualitative data is used when the message (of the analysis) is in the shape (square, circle, triangle) to reveal relationships between multiple values, connect major themes, layer messages (of the analysis) in a systematic manner, and show change over time.

The shaped message (of the analysis) is best displayed in semantic networks word clouds, clusters, trees; hierarchies or information) and storyboarding (text and images).

Revealing relationships between multiple values is best displayed in semantic networks (word clouds, clusters, trees; hierarchies of information).

Connections of major themes are best displayed in cognitive maps (mind maps, concept maps, timelines) and storyboarding (text and images).

Layered messages are best displayed in cognitive maps (mind maps, concept maps, timelines) and storyboarding (text and images).

Showing change over time is best displayed in Spatio-temporal visuals, illustrating across space and time.

Tips to follow for data visualization:
- ✓ Do use the full axis and maintain consistency.
- ✓ Do have your pie chart equal to 100%.
- ✓ Do keep it simple.
- ✓ Do include legends and labels.
- ✓ Do pass the squint test.
- ✓ Do ask for others' opinions.
- ✓ Do test your visualization against a color blindness simulator.
- ✓ Do cite sources when appropriate. Things to avoid for data visualization:
- ✓ Don't use more than six colors (usually).
- ✓ Don't change the color scheme(s) midstream.
- ✓ Don't change chart style midstream.
- ✓ Don't use 3D or blow-apart effects.

- ✓ Don't make users do visual math.
- ✓ Don't include too much information!
- ✓ No narratives—use titles, legends, labels, and images.

For grant applications, quantitative visuals are a better storyteller than qualitative visualizations because qualitative visuals can lose the message. Sometimes data alone tells such visual and intricate stories that limited or no narratives are needed. Complex qualitative data interpretations usually require a higher level of design skill and time-consuming learning curves for optimal execution. Lastly, qualitative messages often use quantitative data.

Another tip is to report by a percentage of the whole. Here is what I mean: Instead of only using the number of clients served, express in terms of the percentage of the total market served. Planning and projections can be clearly communicated to potential funders and can be quite impactful when using evidence to establish a baseline. If 5% of the overall market was served last FY, then the aim of increasing that by 2% is clear. This depicts outcomes and impact, telling the story much more effectively than merely stating the inputs and outputs experienced by the participants and other stakeholders served. Furthermore, offering a baseline of 5% frames the reference to quantify an aim of increasing by 2%.

Infographics often combine qualitative and quantitative concepts. An infographic is a collection of images, charts, and minimal text, giving an easy-to-understand overview of a subject. Infographics use striking, engaging visuals to communicate information succinctly at a glance. They are ideal for marketing and reports, but they are never used as primary visual message conveyance in a grant proposal; use as an attachment only.

Beyond the Grant Proposal –

A grant proposal writer is responsible for submitting compelling, comprehensive, and persuasive proposals. Data and metrics should be a part of all three of those targets. When the process of data collection and analysis is understood, data can be explored without creating complex statistical computations, elaborate surveys or polls, or layered evaluation methods to determine if there is a correlation between two elements that are measured. If there is no correlation, then there is no story, no cause-and-effect to parse. The ability to distinguish this can also help identify outliers, which is vital to evaluating and explaining unanticipated outcomes or impacts. This goes back to knowing what to track so that you can work SMARTer, not harder:

Specific—Only measure what needs to be measured to show successful outcomes and prove impacts; use only the data and metrics significant to the particular grant application.

Measurable—Is the data available for the desired metric and message?

Achievable—Will the metric and how it is measured result in the necessary data for your purpose or the evaluation?

Relevant—The data and metrics should reflect the needs of all stakeholders. Know what the stakeholder groups (including grant funders) value and must know because of the "whys" that are important to stakeholders.

Time-bound—The timelier the data is collected, the sooner the data and results can be communicated, and the more powerful and valuable it is.

The grant proposal writer can be integral in establishing a measurement culture within the organization. A measurement culture is a consistent implementation and use of data, metrics, and evaluation results to increase grant funding, impact, and overall revenue. There are no correlations between the size or budget of an organization and high-performance measurement cultures. The smallest organization, or one-person development department, can attain high achievement levels through the consistent collection and use of data and metrics.

With so many nonprofits doing so much good work, why is there so little change in the condition? Fewer than one-third of nonprofits collect and review precise data necessary to make a positive movement toward eliminating the need for their mission. When an organization can demonstrate a substantial cognizance of how data and metrics prove their impacts and validate their sustainability, the probability of winning grant funding increases exponentially.

Storytelling for Grant Proposals

Storytelling is one of the most overused words in nonprofits today! It is probably used so often because so many parts of a nonprofit's existence rely on communicating about its existence. In the highly competitive grant funding world, your storytelling must stand out from all of the other stories, but how does a standout story get written when most people dread or detest writing? How are stories written to be most advantageous in grant proposals?

Stories are most advantageous when narratives answer, "Why should you care? Why now? Why us?" in the grantmaker's mind. In nonprofit storytelling, the story comprises a focused, fact-based narrative supported by comparative, currently relevant, cited statistics and trends. Compelling, real accounts complemented with a tone of urgency. And the moral of the story, so to speak, is that the story must not only directly connect to and support the organization's ability to respond to that need in the community but directly align with the grantmaker's focus and purpose for funding.

Being a prolific writer is not a skill required for great storytelling in any nonprofit narrative. Knowing the elements of tried and true storytelling is necessary, and recognizing where these elements are found internally and externally is crucial. The tried and true elements of storytelling are setting, characters, plot and conflict, resolution, and the (happy) ending. Here is how each is defined by or found in a nonprofit organization:

- ✓ Setting—The physical location in which the problem exists (area, neighborhood, community, city, state, region, country) OR the current situation of condition (derived from the Needs Statement)
- ✓ Characters—The group receiving services OR the inputs (human, financial, and physical/tangible resources)
- ✓ Plot/Conflict—The description of the organization's mission, programs or projects, and the cause(s) of the problem, including facts and figures as well as anecdotes and testimony

- ✓ Resolution—The experiences created by activities and outputs and leading to outcomes for the characters
- ✓ Happy ending—The impacts (long-term change) experienced by the characters

After identifying these elements for the narrative, the writing is mechanical, taking the reader from Point A to Point B.

1. Write phrases and sentences depicting the physical location where the program/project or other funding need exists. The physical location can be a building, community, specific neighborhood, or group within a community or region. In contrast, the setting can be a situation or condition that exists. Many Needs Statements benefit from utilizing both settings.
2. Write phrases and sentences describing the characters—demographics, characteristics, expected numbers of the group receiving services OR list the inputs. For longer Needs Statements, it is likely to have both sets of characters.
3. Write phrases and sentences explaining how the intended outcomes involving the characters address the mission through the program/project or other funding gaps. The Needs Statement implicitly or explicitly talks about the problem(s) and the underlying cause(s) by addressing the mission.
4. Write phrases and sentences highlighting activities, outputs, and outcomes of the program/project and making logical connections between them using quantitative and qualitative examples. The logical connections portray progress towards the impacts and explain how the characters are positively impacted. This exemplifies improvement in the setting as well.
5. Write phrases and sentences illustrating the intended impacts—the fundamental changes anticipated as a result of the program/project, including the long-term benefits of the program/project. Impacts should be quantified whenever possible. (A word about Impacts: There are no right or wrong impacts.)

Work through the storytelling elements for each narrative in the grant application—

Needs Statements, Program/Project Descriptions, Program/Project Evaluations, and even Budget Narratives. Remember, the setting is the tangible location, the "where." It can also be the current intangible situation of the need. The characters are the "who" and "what." The "who" are the living things receiving services. The characters, from an internal standpoint, are the inputs (the "what") used to implement the activities. The plot and conflict are derived from the Needs Assessment and Statement but are expressed in terms of the "how," "when," and "why" in the story. The resolution is conveyed as the activities, outputs, and outcomes expected as a result of implementing the program/project (or other funding needs). The sunset, or happy ending, is your program's positive impact(s). (The block covering "Logic Models for Grant Proposals" details inputs, activities, outputs, outcomes, and impacts.)

The tried and true storytelling elements in nonprofit work also apply to Cover Letters, Letters of Intent/Inquiry, Executive Summaries, and descriptions for partnerships, volunteers, and in-kind contributions. Use this technique for marketing pieces, 990 narratives, annual reports, and fundraising campaigns as well.

The tried and true elements of good storytelling take the reader smoothly and directly from Point A to Point B, but how does this happen? This is accomplished with transition words and conjunctions. Subtle and not-so-subtle transitions create the ah-hah moments in your favorite novel. The same can happen with grant proposal narratives. Both subtle and blatant transitions connect the setting, characters, plot and conflict, and resolution, leading the reader to the sunset or the happy ending. Do not worry; you do not need to take a refresher course on parts of speech to write amazing stories with this process.

After the phrases and sentences supporting the ask for grant funding are written, polishing the prose is next. Use transition words and conjunctions as part of the polishing. This refining process helps strengthen connections to the heart. Polishing combines phrases and sentences with transition words, relationship words, and conjunctions to reinforce the language that compels giving. Polishing tactfully and strategically inserts adjectives, adverbs, and action words, enhancing the original phrases and sentences.

Transitions transform your sentences from a jagged, indirect route heading to the funders' intellect and emotion on a smooth, straight path to their checkbook. Do your descriptions get in and get out without taking the reader through a rhetorical maze or leave them wondering why you do whatever every other organization does? Transitional words, phrases, and conjunctions, used within paragraphs and between paragraphs, and even between sections of a proposal, straighten the jagged path. Transitions and conjunctions quickly reduce words and characters in first-written versions of phrases and sentences, an added benefit of their use.

It is a balancing act to perfect the right combination of SMART talk and heartstring-tugging. It requires beyond-the-basics verbiage of SMART speech and emotion to maintain that direct message. Unfortunately, no formula or rule tells you how many sentences or words to use for each or either. More important is how you combine the two. This is done with transitions.

We know that having an evidence-based program/project for sustainability in today's nonprofit climate is a must. Evidence implies something scientific or at least structured by fact. Evidentiary prose is usually linked to a hypothesis or the concept of a hypothesis. Transitions in your wording help facilitate this idea of a hypothesis. Transitions imply an if-then scenario is at play. For example, "If our expected outcome through workforce development is a job for someone with a disability, then they will have the income to pay for basics like housing and food." We are providing a provable hypothesis for the grant reviewer, whether or not they realize it. Better storytelling implies the if-then scenario rather than using if-then overtly.

It is easier to connect thoughts and processes through explanation than with bulleted lists, and connections are achieved with transitions. The connections are forged by combining the mundane prose of evidence-based program/project details with language and structure that fosters a lump in the readers' throats. The more substantial the evidence and more compelling the storytelling, the bigger the lumps in the throats. Sorry to be blunt, but lumps transition to dollars.

Keep in mind those lumps in throats can be for impact on individuals or groups OR acknowledgment of an organization's outcomes and impacts too. For example, when reviewing grants, I have been touched by reading about how much thought and care went into finding ways to achieve the impacts desired to relieve real strife in a community.

See, storytelling in the nonprofit world is simple and straightforward! Although not a complete list, here are some transition words and conjunctions with which to get started. (*SMART Money Grant Writing: Ready-to-Use Writing* provides guidance and ready-written phrases and sentences for most nonprofit missions and storytelling.) The emboldened group headings identify the type of word(s) for connecting your original words and phrases, accompanied by suggested transition words for nonprofit narratives:

effect/consequence/result
for this reason
because the
consequently
accordingly
in this case
therefore

agreement/addition/similarity
together with
comparatively
equally important
uniquely
similarly
like, likewise
additionally

conclusion/summary/restatement
in the final analysis
as stated above
given these points
as has been noted
in conclusion, in summary

time/chronology/sequence
immediately
by the time
without delay
as long as, as soon as
from, about

limitation/opposition
conversely
nevertheless
even though, despite
above all
at the same time
otherwise

cause/condition/purpose
if-then
in hope that
given that, provided that
only, only when
due to, owing to
for the purpose of
to, in order to

example/support/emphasis	**space/location/place**
to demonstrate	beyond
to emphasize	further
for instance, for example	between
especially	below
explicitly, in detail	under
to point out	

The emboldened group headings identify the type of word(s) for connecting your original words and phrases, accompanied by suggested **conjunctions** (connector words) for nonprofit narratives:

for	if when
and	even if
as long as	inasmuch as
as soon as	just as now
once	since
provided that	supposing
which	that
incidentally	though
nor	until
but	in fact
or	instead
yet	indeed
so	as a
finally	however
after	likewise
as	whenever
though	whereas
before	wherever
if	meanwhile

correlative (comparative) conjunctions

as / as	sooner / than
neither / nor	either / or not
both / and no	only / but also

In addition to using transitions and conjunctions in your wordsmithing, the Thesaurus is handy to make narratives more thought-provoking. A Thesaurus is a resource of synonyms (similar words that can be used interchangeably) to help create variety and interest in storytelling. Most word processing software has a Thesaurus feature. Use this tool sparingly, though, because too many out-of-the-ordinary words can detract from the message and make the overzealous use of a Thesaurus obvious. One additional cautionary note on using a Thesaurus is that in some instances, changing a word that oft-repeats in a narrative might change the meaning or message. Sometimes the same word simply must be repeated because it is specific to the program/project or need.

Using fewer abstract nouns is better—less is more. Palpable prose draws a reader into the something that moved you, something you saw, something you experienced, something for which you feel passionate. Abstract words can be distracting.

Verbs are not left out of the storytelling conversation. Verbs are action words. Many times in grant proposal writing, the verbs become stale and redundant—predictable. Grant funding is about helping create positive change for the future, and why the action in storytelling is explicitly about the future. Using a variety of verbs in grant proposal writing creates and holds the readers' interest, strengthens the message, clarifies sequence, enhances the qualities of any stakeholder group, and elevates the level of readability.

Transitions, conjunctions, and verbs are parts of speech that help guide storytelling. Adjectives and adverbs are parts of speech that can derail storytelling. Adjectives add qualities and conditions to people, places, and things. Adverbs intensify or calm the action. Storytelling is a balancing act with the right combination of words, phrases, sentences, and paragraphs solidifying the heart-centered connections. Too many good things can disarm the message. Not every person, place, thing, or action needs to be accompanied by a descriptor (an adjective or adverb). Be judicious and thoughtful about the wordsmithing.

Grant proposals are business documents, not creative or memoir writing exercises. More advice on adjectives and adverbs is that they are the easiest to eliminate if the character or word count exceeds the given limit.

We understand that not every person or group of people needs to have descriptors (adjectives). However, the labels and language created by adjectives can be detrimental to a grant proposal but, moreover, diminish the person or group of people they describe. Adjectives repurposed as nouns inappropriately label individuals. These labels diminish the human being and often misrepresent or incorrectly group individuals.

Your grammar teacher taught you that adjectives describe people, places, and things. However, you cannot turn adjectives into nouns—people, places, or things—for any messaging, whether you work in nonprofit or for-profit businesses. Your use of adjectives as nouns for words and in phrases like "the homeless," "the underserved," or "the at-risk" should end today.

When adjectives replace people, people are diminished, and the whole of the person is ignored. Let's use homelessness to make our point. When a person lacks a home, they are experiencing homelessness; they are not "the homeless." Stating that someone is homeless or referring to them as "the homeless" infers that being homeless is the only characteristic defining them. A person can be a student, a mom, an activist, a friend, a husband, or unemployed and not have a home.

Too often in nonprofit work, we are worried about or controlled by word and character counts in our communications, including grant proposals. Yes, "the homeless" has far fewer characters and words than "a person experiencing homelessness" but you need to find other places to reduce the word or character counts. The language matters. As a grant proposal writer or another content creator, if you cannot meet word or character count restrictions without replacing nouns with converted adjectives, maybe you are in the wrong business.

Proprietary to grant applications, replacing nouns with adjectives converted to people, generalizes the situation and the community's needs. It is not enough to state there are people experiencing homelessness, for example. What are the contributing factors and characteristics of the person, group, neighborhood, or constituency experiencing homelessness? There are always secondary and tertiary factors or characteristics, multiple dimensions to every individual.

As another example, "the disabled" has fewer characters and words than "people with disabilities." Having a disability is only one small part of a person who happens to be a wheelchair user, hearing impaired, or suffering from debilitating anxiety. My Mom, a wheelchair user, was an employee, as well as a 4-H club advisor, church youth group leader, writer, mom, sister, wife, Mimi (grandmother), small business owner, and the gracious hostess at many holiday open houses.

Keywords are another valuable tool for wordsmithing. A keyword is a significant word from a title or document used mainly to index content. Incorporate keywords in storytelling as the writing is being done. Remember, most narratives in grant proposals do not change from proposal to proposal unless the content needs to be edited to fit formatting or more closely relate to the funder's focus. If keywords change, update the stories when the piece is reviewed periodically.

Manipulating language and terminology is another excellent tool for evoking emotion while balancing evidence in storytelling. Occasionally manipulating norms of sentence structure and punctuation is part of this. What I mean is that exploiting a phrase or one-word sentence emphasized by punctuation injects rhetorical weight and palaver into a narrative. Like the Thesaurus, this tool is used sparingly to make the reader's most impactful heartstring connections.

Heart-centered connections are effortlessly made when the content is humanized. Choose one or two authentic stories featuring how or why funding the gap for this program/project or other organizational penury betters a living thing that has been diminished or damaged. A variety of stories any nonprofit has to tell will put a "face" to the message. In addition to standard needs and "what we are doing" narratives, one is the founding story. Others are the historical perspective with a "walk down memory lane" and overcoming adversity. Donors, volunteers, board members, and partner stories are equally informative and articulate the nonprofit's vision.

Most importantly, connecting a "face" with an impact is not exploiting those receiving services. Some participants appreciate sharing their stories. It connects heartstrings. People fund people (or other living things like puppies or the environment), not programs/projects. And grantmakers are people. The "face" in the story is depicted through demographics, characteristics, and testimonials, not by attaching a photograph.

The heartstring connections are crucial to creating a tone of urgency necessary in grant proposal writing. They are also integral in squelching, "So what?" as the grant proposal reviewer finishes reading your application. A lack of urgency translates to a lack of return on their investment.

It is obvious why the tone of all narrative sections is essential in a grant proposal. That is why they must be SMART. Ensuring that all grant proposal components emanate a cohesive message strengthens the ask and adds to the nonprofit's credibility. SMART storytelling is:

Specific—Uses quantitative and qualitative research closely related to the organization's mission and activities making a logical case for the intended outcomes and impacts of the grant funding ask

Measurable—Employs facts and figures emphasizing the scope of the problem, scalable to the community; includes expected benchmarks during and after delineated time

Achievable—Structures cause(s) of problem and solution(s) with realistic feasibility based on the organization's capacity and target population interest

Relevant—Applies recent expert data and testimony, significant to outputs and expected outcomes and impacts

Time-bound—Clarifies how the grant award will help achieve the organization's mission and funder's focus during a delineated period

The completed narratives should resemble the organization's logic model in content, addressing all inputs, activities, outputs, outcomes, and impacts. Reviewing from the block on "Logic Models for Grant Proposals," logic model development eliminates much of the narrative because of its columnar format. The logic model shows the plan; the narrative tells the story.

Talking about storytelling is incomplete without mentioning the audience. Grant proposal writing circumvents the define-your-audience process in writing. The audience is known and further defined by guidelines that outline targets and purposes for which the money is awarded and imply values and character. The tone of grant proposals might vary by audience. An academic and scientific audience dictates a more formal or analytical tone than a civic association or family foundation application. The reading level can be checked for the intended audience in the polishing stage of writing—editing and proofreading. Some proofing software edits for the reading level.

Understanding how understanding the audience is beneficial to storytelling and grant proposal writing dates back thousands of years to 385 B.C. and Aristotle. Aristotle's three modes of persuasion are ethos, logos, and pathos. Ethos is about establishing a person's authority to speak on the subject. Logos is their logical argument for their point. And pathos is their attempt to influence an audience. Aristotle suggested that ethos, logos, and pathos combine to make substantial impacts. Aristotle also suggested a process using the three modes to persuade, which includes these five steps:

1. Arouse audience interest
2. Pose a problem or questions that require solving/answering
3. Offer a solution to the problem
4. Describe specific benefits of adopting the course of action
5. Call to action

By you, the grant proposal writer, being a subject-matter expert (ethos), when presenting evidence-based narrative content, the argument will be logical (logos), and the tone should be created as urgent and appeal to emotions (pathos). The five steps closely resemble the tried and true elements of storytelling.

- ✓ Setting—The physical location in which the problem exists (area, neighborhood, community, city, state, region, country) OR the current situation of the condition can be used to arouse interest in the audience, to grab their attention because they have a connection to the setting.
- ✓ Characters—The group receiving services OR the inputs (human, financial, and physical/tangible resources) can be used to arouse interest in the audience,

to grab their attention because they have a connection or empathy for the characters.

- ✓ Plot/Conflict—The description of the organization's mission, programs/projects, and the cause(s) of the problem pose the problem for solving or the question for answering.
- ✓ Resolution—The experiences created by activities and outputs and leading to outcomes for the characters as described in the specific encourages adopting the course of action
- ✓ Happy ending—Impacts (long-term change) experienced by the characters as a result of acting on the call to action (i.e., the grant proposal)

Without getting too philosophical, persuasive rhetoric has been a part of human relationships since the beginning of human history. And in nonprofit fundraising (grant funding or otherwise), persuasion is elemental. Creating powerful stories rather than presenting simple sentences crafts a competitive difference in grant proposal writing.

Polish the Proposal

As with creating much of the content in grant proposals, you do not have to be a prolific writer to compose winning grant applications. Working with basic knowledge of sentence structure, grammar, and punctuation accepted in business communications, sticking to easy-to-read and standard-sized fonts, and avoiding run-on sentences are enough. The basics can be enhanced and polished.

Polishing the proposal is part of grant proposal writing and grants management that no other training will tell you. You can have the most substantial Needs Statement and the most well-thought-out program with masterful evaluation methods than any organization and highly qualified personnel in every seat. However, if a sloppy or unsubstantiated proposal is submitted, those things might not matter. I do not tell many anecdotal stories when I train or present, but this is one anecdote that applies across the board. Before nonprofit work and grant proposal writing, my career was planning and decorating events. I did a lot with balloons. Early on, I heard one industry professional tell her story about starting out and having nothing. She had one pair of pierced pearl earrings (faux pearls at that), and she made sure she wore them to every sales appointment to which she went. She reasoned that if she forgot her earrings and the client noticed pierced ears with no earrings, what attention to detail did that show? It's the little things. She could have built the most stunning bridal arches and centerpieces anywhere, but if the client perceived that she missed details, she would not get hired to create those arches and create those centerpieces. It's the little things.

Some of the little things, the tools that will make the details matter include correcting grammar and punctuation, improving sentence structure, elevating the tone and reading level of your work, and formatting. Select the tools that work best for you and your organization. Grant proposal writing creates niched content. Be mindful that no tool will know the precise context, mission-specific persepctive, or program/project-specific words needed to tell your story. Still, they give the option to accept the suggested correction or maintain the original, possibly intentional content. There are many free and low-cost tools.

Grammarly is cloud-based editing software offering a free platform for the basics and paid options allowing you to edit more advanced issues such as pesky dangling participles, awkward phrasing, subject-verb agreement, and more. Grammarly checks for critical grammar and spelling errors, readability, conciseness, plagiarism, and genre-specific writing style while making vocabulary suggestions. It also reviews punctuation and spelling mistakes. The convenience of uploading documents for editing and downloading the Grammarly-corrected version maintains formatting and eliminates copying and pasting between materials.

The Hemingway Editor for desktop and Hemingway App for electronic devices cut the dead weight from your writing and help you write with power and clarity by highlighting adverbs, passive voice, and dull, complicated words. The convenience of importing and exporting text from documents maintains formatting and eliminates copying and pasting between documents. Once the Editor version is on your desktop or laptop, no internet connection is necessary to refine the grant proposal content. Readability is reported by academic grade level, which is crucial to writing to the right audience.

Fresh eyes are free but only purposeful for readability and message. Do not rely on a human for higher-level editing of writing conventions (unless the human is an experienced editor).

Grammar and punctuation checker features in word processing applications such as Microsoft Word, Publisher, Excel, or PowerPoint are only adequate. Do not rely solely on these edit and correction features. If it did the job thoroughly, there would not be other editing apps.

Create a style guide for the grant proposal writing team. (The style guide should be created with input from all organizational departments and executive staff to set consistency for all messaging.) Whether formal or informal, a style guide outlines the technical aspects of documents and messaging (printed and digital). Font, font sizes for various sections of documents, font color, margins, and even paper size if need be. That way, everyone is on the same page. No pun intended. The grant proposal writer might type in Times Roman and assume everyone else does. The accounting team might like Arial, and the volunteer typing up testimonials might think French Script elucidates the best story. When all of these parts are dropped into one grant proposal, it is a mess that takes time to edit into one consistent style. A style guide will save valuable time and reduce frustration.

PDF creation software is a must-have. PDF is the acronym for Portable Document Format. PDFs are used to distribute read-only documents that preserve the layout of a page. Any content that is not submitted in an online grant application form will be a document. The document might be a fill-in or free form application suitable for printing, submitted digitally, through the mail, fax, or as an attachment. Either way, the document will most likely be accessed digitally. It is crucial that the formatting remains as it was when created, regardless of being accessed digitally or printed. The format must be "frozen." Saving a Word document, Excel spreadsheet, Publisher file, or PowerPoint slide or presentation as a PDF freezes the formatting.

Another benefit of PDFs is managing multiple separate pages or documents for grant proposal attachments. It is acceptable (and advisable) to make the most of it when only one attachment is allowed to be submitted with the application. Most PDF creation tools, such as Adobe Suite components, combine separate pages and documents into one PDF document. By knowing what tools are available, you could include, for example, six letters of support, a list of in-kind contributions, a Memorandum of Agreement, an infographic, and a page of testimonials. These were all separate documents in a shared file. Use a PDF creator to drop them all in, put them in the order needed for most significant influence, and click create PDF. Done. It takes less than two minutes, and it was one uploaded document with plenty of valuable information. (I have submitted these dozens of times and never had a grantmaker question it.)

The Unfunded List is grant proposal writing's best-kept secret. It is a nonprofit of experienced grant reviewers who review the proposal(s) and make skilled recommendations for improvement. The Unfunded List is an excellent tool to gauge your grant proposal writing, but do not rely on it to submit a particular proposal by a deadline.

They accept submissions twice yearly, and it takes about two months to receive the reviewed proposal. There are other grant review services and freelancers as well.

Grantmaker guidelines are a tool. Check the grantmaker guidelines one more time just before submitting the completed proposal. Ensure the grantmaker name and contacts' names are spelled correctly and cited appropriately for titles and accreditations, addresses are up-to-date, all required information is contained in the application components, and double-check that the ask still aligns with the funder focus as it did when the opportunity was first vetted.

Proofread via text-to-speech. The content is read aloud, facilitating stop-correct-continue editing for individual paragraphs or entire documents. When working hours, days, or weeks on a grant proposal, it is easy to miss little details such as omitted words or unintended word tense. Hearing the content read aloud likely catches these errors. There are free and fee-based text-to-speech programs.

Having a few trusted tools to polish the proposal will help your work SMARTer, not harder:

Specific—Polishing the proposal ensures targeted content for a specific audience focused on an identified result.

Measurable—Editing and proofreading assess a grant proposal's technical and qualitative aspects, allowing for message evaluation before submission.

Achievable—Editing software can elevate the content and conveyance to the exact tone prescribed in the tool's parameters to achieve the intended persuasive message.

Relevant—Not every grant application requires the use of all editing and proofing tools. Implement the one(s) pertinent to the content and format.

Time-bound—Editing and proofing for the final draft must be deadline-driven, or the process will be never-ending because writers (grant proposal or otherwise) are seldom satisfied with their work.

Polishing the grant proposal can leave a lasting impression on the grantmaker because error-free applications demonstrate attention to detail, validate advocacy, and respect the grantmaker's time. And remember, a polished grant proposal is a sales proposal, a logical call to action, and a catalyst for relationships—not *For Whom the Bell Tolls*! A grant proposal writer understands that persuasive messaging goes far beyond words.

Research Resources for Grant Proposal Content

I could write a book on resources and research for grant proposal content! Although there are not endless resources, there are copious amounts for grant applications. Because *SMART Money Grant Writing* is about making grant proposal writing SMART, this block will impart reliable resources to improve grant proposal writing and where to find trustworthy research to create evidence-based and compelling content. (The block on "Finding and Vetting Grants" covers resources for finding funding opportunities.)

While formatting and submitting grant applications improve vastly with technology advances, writing content has not fared as well. Before the internet and Google searches, resources were found in libraries, academic papers, newspapers, and periodicals—thumbing through pages and pages for hours on end. However, resources (i.e., printed pages) could be effortlessly limited to a couple of newspapers, encyclopedias, government reports, or academic dissertations. And for the most part, the trustworthiness of printed resources was more discernable. Today, one internet search results in tens of thousands of possibilities that are not necessarily sorted by integrity or relevance of the keyword used to search.

- Here are some general guidelines to manage the initial massive search and its results:
- Limit the number of reliable resources for any program/project or other funding need for which a grant proposal is written to no more than five.
- Maintain a list of these resources, including names, dates published, and website links.
- Develop a system for finding the information necessary for the grant proposal content.
- Pick one style for citations of resources (MLA, APA, *Chicago Manual of Style* are a few), and use it across the organization. Create a citation cheat sheet.

- The analysis and findings from facts and figures should be less than three years old.

Remember, these are general guidelines for the typical program/project and small- and mid-sized nonprofits. These are also relevant to for-profit businesses and individuals (writers, artists, and others) applying for grant money.

Research for grant proposal content is an entirely separate topic from researching grant opportunities. It is just as crucial to a successful grants strategy, however. Because it is nearly impossible for the program/project to be an entirely new idea, authority and credibility must be established with evidence and a thorough understanding of the community's need and cause(s). Evidence requires authoritative citation.

In most cases, it is crucial to understand that you are not conducting research. Instead, you are finding pertinent facts and figures from higher-level research conducted by others. These relevant facts and figures are then woven into narratives to explain the need, support the reason for grant funding in Program/Project Descriptions, justify budget items, compare program/project impacts or expected impacts, and offer summative clarifications in Executive Summaries or Cover Letters. Most of us are not trained to conduct research that involves identifying a question, gathering information, analyzing and evaluating evidence, drawing conclusions, and sharing the knowledge gained in a scientific or social-scientific manner. (An organization might conduct research in its evaluation processes, or if conducting research is its primary activities, the majority of nonprofits do not conduct high-level research.) The most persuasive narratives are bolstered by expertise. Although commitment and compassion have a place in nonprofit work, they do not make most of us experts.

Research integrated into grant proposals serves two purposes:
1. Establishes conditions in the target community or population
2. Documents the need of the nonprofit's clients

Nearly every component of a grant proposal uses research on some level. The research can come from internal resources (within the organization) and is found most of the time externally. Seldom will your research be conducted as a new study. The research interpreted for proposal content is undertaken by higher-level studies and analysis than most organizations have the capacity to do. It is acceptable and expected that primary and secondary resources are found in various places. A nonprofit will incorporate scientific and social scientific research into its proposal content. The primary, secondary, and tertiary resources are part of the recommended five reliable resources, most of which will be secondary.

Internal resources are also referred to as primary resources. Unless the organization is a research institute, most of the (internal) primary research your organization conducts will be for evaluation and reporting. The primary research to be used are original materials on which other research is based. This is the internally generated facts and figures, usually derived from tracking and evaluating inputs, activities, outputs, outcomes, and impacts.

Secondary research sources are most commonly used for grant application narratives, charts and tables, and even infographics and are found externally (outside the organization). Secondary research is information synthesized and analyzed from others' research—books, articles, whitepapers, and more—which have been interpreted and applied from their studies, investigations, or fieldwork.

Tertiary resources, also external, are used to find and organize primary and secondary resources, such as indexes, abstracts, and databases. Separately, they often further explain or support information found in secondary resources.

So, what are the reliable evidentiary resources for grant proposal content?

- Government—federal, state, county, and municipality
- Research organizations—clinical/medical, market, social, scientific
- Libraries—public, government, college alumni system
- White papers, Concept papers
- Academic journals
- Textbooks, reference materials
- Nonpartisan, unbiased newspapers
- Nonprofit periodicals and newsletters
- Following are a few reliable research sources, in no particular order:

- U.S. Census Bureau, Community Report
- data.gov
- city-data.com
- Community foundations studies and reports
- National and state advocacy organizations and associations—Example: Disability Rights Ohio
- Chambers of Commerce
- Professional associations
- National Center on Charitable Statistics
- Federal and state health policy institutes or agencies
- Human Services Research Institute
- Social Work Policy Institute Librarians
- Library guides
- MIT Poverty Action Lab
- Feeding America

(*This list is not intended to endorse general or specific resources.)

As we said, we cannot have an entirely new idea. How the research is used to support or frame the need will help show the unique twist the program/project puts on the approach to solving or improving the problem. Similarly, the presentation of research is useful in grant proposals. For example, a list can be formatted in a box within an application to break up lengthy narratives; bulleted lists work best for this feature. The same can be done with expert quotes or testimonials.

Miscellany about positioning research in grant applications:

- Government grant proposals are data-heavy and require relevant current evidence and accurate citations.
- In non-government grant proposals, citations can be narrative: "According to the 2019 Allsup Study, people with disabilities who are working experience decreased reliance on public services and increased enjoyment of life."
- Use the footnote method of citing (for tables) as it does not need to follow

APA or MLA, etc.
- Weave statistics into narratives: "XYZ town has high poverty rates, with 23.4% of area residents living below the poverty line."
- Tables and charts should have context. Use a narrative introduction to a table or graph to provide context. Here is an example: "The communities our job and career development programs serve are characterized by low income, unemployment, and high poverty (Table X below). Annual per capita income is $9,100 less than the national level, and unemployment is consistently high. The result is almost one-quarter of all XYZ County residents with disabilities have incomes below the poverty level." The context helps establish a tone of urgency.
- Wikipedia is not considered a reliable resource for evidence.
- Social determinants are crucial to data and research for many nonprofit missions.

There are SMART ways to narrow the overwhelming search for facts and figures to relativize grant proposal content. And even though few ideas are original, most can be backed by evidence. Seek out SMART research:

Specific—Facts and figures demonstrating the need and supporting the activities addressing the needs with resultant impacts

Measurable—Qualitative and quantitative information that scale to the need of the community

Achievable—Utilizes reliable resources to obtain primary, secondary, and tertiary research

Relevant—Employs reliable, qualified resources to demonstrate need and support the response to the need in the community

Time-bound—No more than three (3) years old

Research is part of the grant proposal writing process. Whether the grant proposal writer finds the research on appropriate data to make a case for funding effectively or another team member does, research is the foundation upon which a well-described, well-reasoned, compelling, and rigorous proposal content is built. Additionally, research from reliable resources supports the nonprofit's unique program/project designed from new understandings with innovative approaches to alleviate the problem. Research and reliable resources, when used robustly, are perhaps the most valuable tool a grant proposal writer possesses.

Tarra Nystrom

Managing the Grant Proposal Writing Process

Grants Management

It might be argued that every block in the *SMART Money Grant Writing* is about grants management. However, from start to finish, a few principal aspects of managing the grant process have less to do with writing and more to do with cyclical, ongoing activities.

Grants management should be approached much like project management—leading (a team) to achieve grant funding targets and meet success criteria in a specific time. A grant proposal writer's skill set, beyond the writing itself, involves coordinating knowledge, skills, tools, people, and techniques to accomplish the grant portion of the funding strategy. The management process should follow all organizational policies and procedures applicable to grant funding or fundraising. Larger nonprofits will have more formal and informal policies than smaller nonprofits.

The funding strategy must be comprehensive. A comprehensive grants management system helps track grant performance, keep stakeholders up-to-date, and improve data collection and compiling reports. A complete system ensures compliance with reporting requirements, from financial updates to progress checks with funders. It reduces inefficiency by spending less time tracking data. Mismanagement can result in losing grant revenue and not being awarded future grants. In rare cases, it can result in repaying part or all of the original award.

The word tracking is synonymous with grants management. It probably appears in every block in this book. It is safe to assume that something is tracked at every step in the grant process. How whatever is tracked is tracked is crucial to overseeing this part of a nonprofit. These include grant opportunities, various soft and hard deadlines, program/project data and metrics, documents, content, budgets, and more. There are valuable tools to manage these parts and pieces efficiently.

Perhaps the most practical tool is a calendar. Calendars should be continually updated with soft and hard deadlines for:

- Grant submissions, including a timeline for all components of the process Grant reporting (progress and final reports)
- Meetings including invitees and purpose(s)
- Internal targets including departmental content submissions (Program/Project Descriptions, Budgets, Executive Summaries, Program/Project Evaluations, and Volunteer Value) and volunteer contributions
- External targets such as partnership and collaboration contributions
- Assign soft deadlines in advance of hard deadlines for optimal results. A soft deadline reminds you to remind yourself or other people on the team about looming hard deadlines. Assign hard deadlines a few days ahead of the absolute deadline. There is nothing wrong with submitting a grant application a few days before the funder's deadline. In fact, that should be the expectation every time; not waiting until the last minute reduces stress.
- Electronic calendars are easily shared to schedule, send, and accept meeting notifications. Whether publicly shared or planned for one's own purpose, calendar tasks always need to include the point person(s) or organization(s).

The timetable (also a tool) for a particular grant and the grants strategy are also posted on the calendar. It is essential to understand the time involved with each step in the process and component of the application. Here is a sample of steps to track:

- Find grant opportunities—Ongoing opportunity research helps maintain a consistent and robust grant funding strategy; schedule one to two hours monthly.
- Vet each identified opportunity—It is better to spend more time on the front end of vetting each grant opportunity to prioritize it or eliminate it and move on if the grantor is not a fit. Plan a minimum of 15 to 20 minutes for each possible grant award; 30 minutes to an hour for some government RFPs.
- Prep grant applications—Save or create a copy of the application as a working copy of a word processing document, preventing loss of content or accidentally submitting it before it is completed. This only takes five to ten

minutes.

- Writing the proposal—Every grant proposal is different, and timeframes will vary from two hours to two months. Inventory the funder-required components and attachments, then compare the list to what is already written and available. Estimate the time to allow for writing a particular proposal based on the results of this process. Allow ample time for others on the grant proposal writing team to coordinate their assigned writing tasks.

- Composing and editing proposal content—Schedule uninterrupted time to write. The volume of proposals, the size of the team, and submission deadlines dictate the amount and frequency of blocked time but start with at least four to six hours weekly.

- Keep a copy of the submitted information—Saving the content in each proposal takes one to two minutes but saves immeasurable time later if asked to revise the proposal or access the content (including such content edited for the word or character count for future applications).

- Submission—A few seconds, usually to click "Submit." Submitting by email could take as long as five minutes to write a cover-letter style email to introduce the application.

- Waiting for the decision—The typical decision date is 60-90 days after the deadline to submit. As with many other things in grant proposal writing, the decision timeframe varies from grant to grant.

- Award notification to "cash-in-hand"—Again, this varies from grant to grant. Some funders use Electronic Funds Transfer to deposit funds for use immediately. Others send a check or want to schedule a check presentation. A few are structured as reimbursement grants. A standard timeframe is no more than a week after the announcement for most awarded grants.

- Post-award reporting—The grantmaker's guidelines frequently specify the reporting expectations and include progress and end-of-program/project funding period. If there is no required progress and/or final reporting, write a one-page letter to the funder immediately after the funding period ends (within seven days). Express gratitude and highlight the return on investment of their money (outputs, outcomes, and impacts). Progress reports are usually submitted quarterly but sometimes monthly. Unless otherwise stated, the end-of-program/project funding period reports should be submitted within one month of the funding period's end. Set soft deadlines for the team to finalize their reporting to provide final reports on time. The time required for progress and post-award reporting varies from grant to grant, but plan one or two hours each time a report is due.

- Grants funding strategy—Plan for and limit the team to one month for creating an initial grant funding strategy. Similarly, plan for and limit the team to a set deadline (best when in coordination with budget deadlines) for reviewing and updating the annual grants strategy. The grants funding strategy should include the working Grants Tracker (regardless of its format, printed or digital spreadsheet). The opportunities on the Tracker should be reviewed and re-prioritized quarterly. This review involves a comparison with recently updated funding gaps. The executive and accounting staffs are part of this task. Plan an hour or two monthly, at minimum, for this step of the process.
- Grants department update for internal partners—A monthly report on the grants department's status or approach demonstrates the grant proposal writer's value to the organization and board. A dashboard showing (fiscal) year-to-date grant amounts applied for, awarded, restricted/unrestricted, and an abbreviated narrative on two or three notable submissions takes no more than 30 minutes to create initially and less than 15 to update and distribute monthly. Use the update to remind board members, key staff, and well-networked volunteers to help influence pending/future decisions of grantmakers with whom they have professional or personal connections; mark the calendar for follow-up.

Another indispensable tool for grants management is the team. The team members are critical to grant success, but the grant proposal writer is ultimately responsible for the overall grants program and strategy. The team members of one application or all applications can be internal and external. The internal team members are individuals working within the entire nonprofit or in a department. The nonprofit's size and scope will dictate the size of the grant proposal writing staff and the internal team supporting grant efforts. The external members might comprise partners, collaborators, research sources, or community experts. The team does not include the grantmaker. (Communication with a grantmaker only occurs if there is a specific question about a guideline, ascertaining the spelling of a name associated with the submission, or verifying an address. Relationship building with the grantmaker does not happen during the grant submission process.)

Communication with the team is as critical as the team members. For grant proposal writing purposes, permit yourself to be the boss and manage the team. That does not imply being bossy. Although these tips should be common sense, reminders can be helpful:

- ✓ Solicit information with "please" and "thank you"—do not beg, demand, or whine.
- ✓ Emails and meetings must provide succinct requests for narratives, bulleted lists, data and metrics, and budgets, including keeping the grant proposal writer updated on significant changes to programs/projects and budgets.
- ✓ Documents, graphics, photos, templates, and other information are kept current in the grants section of the organization's shared-filed system.
- ✓ Set hard deadlines in writing for others in advance of your own.
- ✓ Chocolate, always have chocolate.

Regardless of the team's size and scope, the software can be a tool the whole team uses. Fortunately, a range of software and technology solutions will help meet demands and grow with the program/project or organization. Grants management software tools, usually included with fundraising or donor data software, can provide the following benefits:

- Search for relevant grant opportunities in an updated database
- Reduce paperwork
- Track grant applications

- Store frequently used documents and organization information
- Offer accounting support and tracking
- Provide real-time updates on projects, resources, and financials
- Improve team collaboration and communication
- Solicit success stories to demonstrate the impact of the program/project

Whether software or manual systems are utilized, the award must be managed. In most cases, immediately or within a few days of submitting a proposal, the funder will notify the nonprofit that the application has been received. It is ok to reach out to the funder to confirm receipt of the application if no confirmation followed the submission. It does not hurt to take a screenshot of the confirmation if one pops up after clicking " submit. If the application is submitted through email, the date stamp on the sent communication will serve as confirmation. There is no reason to add reporting deadlines to the calendar tool until an award has been affirmed.

The best tool for post-award management is communication. When the award is confirmed is the time to add reporting and related deadlines for the particular grant to the calendar. This is also the time to let all internal and external parties involved with post-award management (spending and reporting) know that the grantmaker selected the funding request and notify these parties of the assigned deadlines and responsibilities associated with money. Ongoing communication regarding how and when the funding is used is critical to the grant proposal writer for compliance with what was presented on the proposal and agreed upon by accepting the money. Timely communication, as alluded to, will ensure progress and final reporting are completed to grantmaker expectations and requirements.

A tool that is begrudgingly added to grants management is a process to handle declined asks. Most grant asks are not granted. Remember, only between 10% and 20% of asks are awarded. Disappointment is natural, but do not dwell on it. Here are some suggestions for managing declines:

- Do not internalize the loss. It is part of the profession.
- If no reviewer notes or reasoning accompany the rejection notice, politely ask the grantmaker how the proposal could have been more persuasive and ask if

a revised proposal should be submitted during their next funding cycle.
- Sometimes the program/project or other funding need did not align closely enough; if the decline was an alignment issue, there is no sense in re-applying.
- Some declines result from funds running out before your proposal was reviewed.
- Sometimes the competition was simply better.
- There are likely reviewer comments for government grant proposals. Ask for a copy if they were not sent.
- For local or regional declines, implement additional relationship-building by inviting the grantmaker to tour the facility and see the programs/projects in action.
- Recalibrate the grants search to identify a new list of foundation and corporate funders for grant requests to fill the gap.
- Submit samples of grant applications to grant reviewers to gauge grant proposal writing skills. There are paid and unpaid options for these evaluations.
- Perform an internal audit of the proposal if expectations were exceptionally high for the particular award. Was it carefully matched to the foundation's interests? Did it overreach on geographical location? Did it overextend on the amount of money requested?

Perusing quality sample and completed proposals (written at various levels) is a tool for gaining constructive insight. Reading other proposals imparts perception from what others write, comparative analysis of skill levels, tone, and so much more.

The last tool is chocolate. Yes, chocolate. Do not underestimate its power, not just as a stress reliever but as a management tool. Placing a bowl of chocolate treats on the front corner of your desk is a subtle invitation to grant team members to "come on in." The bowl of chocolate provides a casual yet deliberate means to mention a pending deadline or discuss content that is not coming together as hoped or intended. Chocolate doubles as a reward too! (My advice is to fill the bowl with pieces you do not like to refrain from consuming it all.)

There are non-financial benefits of grants management as well. Management implies focusing on (or bringing back into focus) key aspects required for success. The various modes of grants management focus attention on consolidating or organizing programs/projects and processes, generating new ideas, streamlining workflow, developing new collaborations, training or orienting new staff or volunteers, and keeping the big picture in view.

In the same light as giving yourself permission to be the grant team's boss, permit yourself to be human. The most significant reason why humans fail to plan is the fear of failure. There are no absolutes in life or grant proposal writing. So, stop expecting absolutes and perfection. The deterrents to planning start with "should-ing" ourselves: "I should be doing this, or I should have done that."

Next are the self-imposed expectation of perfection and the rigidity of attempting to achieve perfection. Grant proposal writing is complex, and the feeling of inadequacy can creep in. Finally, unjustifiable ideas of Imposter Syndrome have been known to overtake the most experienced grant proposal writers. Self-doubt hits everyone at one time or another, overriding any feelings of success or external proof of competency. Humans achieve and succeed so much more often than they fail. Grant proposal writing is much the same. Self-care is a great management tool to add to your arsenal.

Managing grants that fuel the organization can be a demanding, complicated process pervaded with meetings, paperwork, and deadlines. However, it can be straightforward and free from stress. More grant money is won, additional collaborations are created, and stronger, non-transactional relationships are built if grants management is SMART. This eliminates burdens allowing focus on the top priority: fulfilling the mission of the organization.

Specific—Identify funding needs, plausible grant opportunities, and internal and external team members.

Measurable—Identify the percentage of the budget to identify grant money, translate to the dollar amount.

Achievable—Identify grant opportunities closely aligning the funding gaps, mission, award timeframe, and capacity with the grantmaker's focus and guidelines.

Relevant—Do not apply for a grant because the focus merely has one or two keywords matching the program/project. The grant must be well-aligned and thoroughly vetted.

Time-bound—An ongoing and consistent strategy allows for the replacement or rotation of grant support to sustain programs/projects or secure other crucial resources for the nonprofit's sustainability.

Wellness for Grant Proposal Writing Professionals

Working in a nonprofit is rewarding. Whether nonprofit work is intentional or fallen into, the pros outweigh the cons. However, as with most jobs and careers, nonprofit work is stressful. Grant proposal writing has a unique set of stressors, but none are unmanageable. Self-care is crucial to healthy, balanced lives. The words *deadline*, *strategy*, *writing*, *team*, *decline*, and others associated with grants can make even the most seasoned nonprofit professional a little tense.

Self-care is subjective. Just as no two grant applications are alike, no two grant proposal writers' self-care are alike. Essentially, self-care requires one to relax, recharge, and reinvigorate. Working and volunteering in a nonprofit is stressful. The hours can be demanding, combined with wanting and being tasked to get as much done as possible in the allotted time.

Grant proposal writers owe it to themselves, their families, and all stakeholder groups from constituents to the Board of Directors to find and implement a workable work-life balance. Last-minute, half-assed efforts are not a prudent use of donor dollars. Self-care is about physical, mental, and emotional well-being to manage time and stress. Time management and stress management are not mutually exclusive.

The physical aspects of self-care are easier to accomplish than the mental and emotional ones—getting enough sleep, maintaining a healthy diet, and exercising regularly. This is not merely about productivity or a bubbly personality in the workplace. Sleep, diet, and exercise make life more enjoyable for you and those closest to you.

The mental and emotional pieces take scrupulous attention and even practice to create relaxing, recharging, and reinvigorating habits. We have come to view relaxing as a shortcoming or something we should feel guilty about doing. In reality, relaxation benefits the individual doing it and might be more beneficial to those in contact with the person practicing relaxation skills. Just 15 minutes a day with a favorite magazine, cup of tea, or other self-perceived self-indulgence improves mental and emotional well-being. During the workday, leave your desk (and building) for lunch, connect for a few minutes with a volunteer in a non-nonprofit conversation, take a 10-minute walk before the final proposal edit, or retreat for a few minutes of deep breathing after a spirited meeting are a few suggestions.

We are lost when the battery of our phone dies. Grant proposal writers need to recharge just as batteries do, or the organization will be at a loss. Recharging can be as quick as something mentioned for relaxing or as long as a day or weeks away from the workplace. Personal and sick time are strategic parts of human resources policies and handbooks. The executive staff and the board of directors appreciate the value of paid time off to have it included in employee benefits. Be strategic in self-care and use that time. On the rare occasion that more time is necessary, negotiating unpaid leave can be advantageous to the employee and the nonprofit.

A day off or a brisk walk can certainly reinvigorate. Reinvigoration can be energy to finish the day, a fresh perspective, or a new project (work-related project, not a new program/project for the targeted constituency). Maybe now is the time to pitch a new area for grant funding or a different evaluation method to improve a program/project and post-award grant reporting. Routine is necessary and valuable but can turn to monotony. Fresh perspectives and revised aspirations (such as new work projects) will break the monotony.

When relaxing, recharging, and reinvigorating are innate, resilience follows. Resilience means that you will understand stress triggers and automatically control them—well, at least do what is in your power to manage them. Resilience means burnout is far in the rearview mirror. Resilience is a result of SMART self-care:

Specific—Self-care is personal and individual. Only you can identify distinctive ways to relax, recharge, and reinvigorate.

Measurable—A quick personal assessment of how you feel before a bit of self-care and after will reveal the difference in your mindset and energy level.

Achievable—Self-care is personal and individual. Only you can identify distinctive ways to relax, recharge, and reinvigorate that work for you.

Relevant—Self-care to relax, recharge, and reinvigorate results in resilience.

Time-bound—Self-care is habit-forming. Make it a daily habit.

As a grant proposal writer and trainer, I cannot prescribe how every other grant proposal writer should self-care. I am not formally trained as a counselor, therapist, or in mindfulness. I can only emphasize the importance of managing time and stress as a grant proposal writer to help you experience your best life. I can tell you to practice deep breathing or mindfulness daily, but that is not my expertise or place. (I find checking my favorite retailer's site for great bargains does as much for me as yoga!) I can only declare that taking a little bit of my day for **me** improved my writing, increased my productivity, positively impacted my tolerance, made me a more vital part of the team, and allowed for tactical juggling of competing priorities in my life. I guess taking a little bit of my day for me helped me avoid burnout over time.

SMART self-care proves valuable:

Specific—Improve your writing.

Measurable—Increase your productivity.

Achievable—Allow for tactical juggling of competing priorities in your life.

Relevant—Positively impact your tolerance, making you a more vital part of the team.

Time-bound—Help you avoid burnout over time.

With all of that said, if consulting or freelancing is preferred over traditional grant proposal writing roles, self-care of relaxing, recharging, and reinvigorating includes boundaries. Just because on a particular afternoon or weekend, a client decides "now is the time to tackle this" and wants answers NOW, it does not mean that the professional (i.e., you, their contracted grant proposal writer) from whom they need those answers is available or works 24/7/365. Remember, as a contractor, you are not part of the inner circle. Those more casual and personal relationships they share with their inner circle do not immediately extend to partners and consultants. You are the boss of your time, and it is okay to establish business boundaries:

- Typical business hours are 9-5, M-F (unless otherwise stated or established by a working relationship. A working relationship is not created by one handshake or the fact that you have their business card.)

- Do not text unless you have established that protocol with the client.
- Allow and establish a 24-hour timeframe to respond to a message, email, text, or voicemail. There will be emergencies or deadline-related communication; these are exceptions, not the rule.

As a consultant, I received texts at 10:15 pm asking if it is a good time to talk. No, it is not. A voicemail early Saturday morning demanding a call back as soon as I get the message. Huh? Three emails in two hours; the subsequent ones ask why I haven't responded yet. Really? Being a consultant does not mean being on call for clients around the clock (unless the consultant chooses). Even some traditional employer-employee relationships cross the line with that expectation. Business boundaries are for self-care and sanity.

In the same light as permitting yourself to be the boss of the grants management team, permit yourself to be human—the most significant reason humans burn out is a lack of self-care. There are no absolutes in life or grant proposal writing. So, stop expecting absolutes and perfection. The beginnings of burnout start with "should-ing" ourselves—"I should be doing this, or I should have done that."

Next are the self-imposed expectation of perfection and the rigidity of attempting to achieve perfection. Grant proposal writing is complex, and the feeling of inadequacy can creep in. Finally, unjustifiable ideas of Imposter Syndrome have been known to overtake the most experienced grant proposal writers. Self-doubt hits everyone at one time or another, overriding any feelings of success or external proof of one's competence. Humans achieve and succeed so much more often than they fail. Contracted and freelance grant proposal writers are humans, and grant proposal writing is much the same. There are truly only two things in life over which we have no choice—death and taxes.

When you permit yourself to make real choices—YOUR choices—you are genuinely self-caring. The choices are not always going to be what you want or expect. Desires and expectations are great. But the world will not stop revolving if some of those desires or expectations get re-routed. So stop should-ing all over yourself and beating yourself up when a re-route occurs. I taught you to breathe in the block on "Logic Models" when logic models seemed incredibly scary and impossible. Now, practice that in all the other parts of your grant proposal writing world!

Hiring and Being Hired as A Grant Proposal Writer

Grants are an integral and lucrative part of any nonprofit funding strategy. And grant proposal writing, good grant proposal writing, is valued in most nonprofits. Hiring and being hired as a grant proposal writer is more than demonstrating sentence structure skills or knowing where to find grant opportunities. Becoming an experienced grant proposal writer entails sharpening a variety of skills and honing particular traits.

Grant proposal writing as a career offers two options—traditional employment and freelance or consulting. Regardless of the career path, the following is how a grant proposal writer becomes successful:

- An experienced grant proposal writer is cost-effective, focused, and adept with proposal saturation and diversification.
- An experienced grant proposal writer meets deadlines every time. A professional grant proposal writer prepares the proposal with ample time for review and revisions well ahead of the submission deadline.
- An experienced grant proposal writer has a practical understanding of multiple funding opportunities and formats and online grants management systems.
- An experienced grant proposal writer knows what is required to complete a comprehensive submission, even if the organization is not grant-ready.
- An experienced grant proposal writer conducts research and prioritizes funding opportunities based on that research AND the organization's funding strategy and capacity.
- An experienced grant proposal writer interviews key organizational leaders and staff to become familiar with the mission, program/project, history, and funding gaps of the nonprofit rather than assuming all information is the same across the nonprofit world.

- An experienced grant proposal writer is an active listener.
- An experienced grant proposal writer is willing and available to follow through to the reporting stage of the funding partnership.
- An experienced grant proposal writer has strong business writing skills that complement effective storytelling competencies.
- An experienced grant proposal writer is a proficient proofreader and editor.
- An experienced grant proposal writer is curious, detailed-oriented, and results-driven.
- An experienced grant proposal writer is willing to suggest if a grant opportunity might be inappropriate for the organization. Inappropriateness can be based on too large of an ask or, on rare occasions, if the grantmaker is controversial or has a less-than-favorable reputation.

Being hired as a grant proposal writer –

As a traditionally employed grant proposal writer, you have a couple of choices. It depends upon what you want to do. If you wish to write grant proposals only, then targeting a large organization with a bigger development team with dedicated grant proposal writer positions is the best choice. With smaller organizations (one- to three-person development teams), you will wear more fundraising hats than just grant proposal writing.

To be able to write grant proposals and manage the grant process solely, you want to be part of the development team. That role would include researching grant opportunities, vetting and prioritizing grant opportunities based on the funding gap of the program/project or other funding need (such as technology, volunteer initiatives, capital projects, staff or professional development, to name a few), researching grant proposal content, writing and submitting the grant proposals, and reporting post-award.

If you are part of a smaller team or one-person office, you will likely have multiple responsibilities. In addition to grant proposal writing and management (as described above), you would be expected to work with:

- ✓ Individual donors
- ✓ Corporate partnerships

- ✓ Civic and faith partnerships
- ✓ Sponsorships (event and/or other)
- ✓ Fundraising events
- ✓ In-kind Donations
- ✓ Year-end, mid-year, and/or capital campaigns
- ✓ Database management
- ✓ and possibly more

Working in a role as a development manager or development director certainly involves grant proposal writing and grants management, but it also involves sales, networking, and much relationship-building. If you are comfortable with sales and networking and desire to do that, then working in a smaller office will allow for grant proposal writing and other fundraising outreach.

Working as a consultant or freelancer –

Being a grant proposal writing consultant or freelancer provides much flexibility and variety as a career. Some "musts" as a contracted employee are contracts, confidentiality agreements, a reasonable hourly rate or package pricing, a user-friendly and engaging website, timely accounting and bookkeeping habits, and most importantly, strict adherence to industry ethics standards. Some considerations as a contracted employee are working by retainer, setting regular hours for client meetings and communication, using time tracking software for each client, and using a CPA for bookkeeping and tax reporting.

If you join or already work with an organization with a mission for which you have not executed grant proposal writing in the past, make sure you are fully oriented on its operations. How can you effectively and persuasively fundraise without fully understanding how the organization works?

You can also work as a grant reviewer. However, reviewing is usually not full-time work. Government agencies and grant-making foundations (corporate and community) often pay skilled grant reviewers. There are also volunteer grant reviewing opportunities. Grant reviewing proffers occasions to see what grantmakers are looking for in proposals; their rubrics can be very illuminating. For additional insights into grant scoring rubrics, perform an internet search of such. It will improve your grant proposal writing skills.

Compensation for grant proposal writers varies with experience, award success, size of the nonprofit, and location. Compensation should never be based on dollars awarded or a percentage of awarded proposals. Dollars and percentages awarded are relative and do not always indicate experience or success. Separately, an important thing to know about grant proposal writers' compensation is that it must be hourly or a salary. It is unethical to be compensated with a commission or percentage of a grant award. In some states, it is illegal. Some organizations do not know about this illegality, although they should, and some that do try to skirt the system. Some nonprofits advertise for a grant proposal writer with compensation by commission or percentage. These organizations should be ignored or interviewed by letting them know you would need an hourly rate or a salary.

A freelance grant proposal writer or consultant can expect to juggle many aspects of a business. Client meetings, office administration, marketing and selling, continuing education, and accounting will compete for time to write.

A freelancer or consultant must consider what type of billing works best for them. Some of the choices are invoicing for time (an hourly rate), materials, and travel at an agreed-upon interval (typically monthly), obtaining a retainer, charging a flat fee per grant service or package, and value-based billing (based on the consultant's knowledge in the market place). All billing, fees, and service details should be formally agreed upon between client and consultant with a contract. Time tracking software can provide transparency to the client that hours worked and expenses accrued are accurate and necessary.

It is okay to negotiate payment of particular office expenses directly associated with a client's grants management. Postage and shipping costs can add up quickly. Consider that although few applications are mailed or shipped now, the printing costs can be significant when (for example) the grantmaker requests three copies of the application and attachments. A 990 or audit can be dozens of pages. Mailing or shipping such a packet with tracking numbers or other specialized options might be $10-$30 or more.

When beginning a consultancy of grant proposal writing, it is tempting to discount rates and package pricing to secure those first few clients. This is a bad precedent for a couple of reasons. Cheap begets cheap and implies a lack of experience or credibility, not only for the grant proposal writer but also for the client. You know your value as a grant professional, or you would not (and should not) be selling grant proposal writing services. Significant discounts diminish your value and that of every other grant proposal writer. Instead, find an incentive rate or package pricing for marketing, such as $10 off the hourly rate or 25% off a package purchased by a specific date. Incentives are also appropriate to extend courtesies for client referrals. For example, "My hourly rate is $75. However, because Dan and I work closely together and he put us in contact with each other, I am happy to offer you $65 an hour." Understand if this new client is locked in at $25 an hour, that is where that billing rate will stay. It is nearly impossible to raise a low starter rate to a standard rate. In nonprofits, as in for-profit businesses, it takes money to get money. Nonprofit administrators and boards of directors must understand the value of investing in you.

If you choose to volunteer your time and talents as a grant proposal writer, you can take advantage of tax deductions allowable in your state and with the IRS, such as mileage reporting, business expenses, or other benefits. Be selective. Ensure the organization is reputable and transparent. Follow all Conflict of Interest policies of the nonprofit and those that might apply to your regular job or career.

Throughout *SMART Money Grant Writing*, you have probably noticed consistent use of the phrase "grant proposal writer" rather than "grant writer." We write and submit grant proposals. Therefore, we are grant proposal writers. Grant writers are on the funder's end, writing the instructions and other information about the grant award. It sounds like a little thing, but when I heard someone else say it, it made so much sense, and I have adopted this thinking.

Hiring a grant proposal writer –

When making grant proposal writer hiring decisions, you should:
- Consider a freelance grant proposal writer or independent contractor rather than adding an employee to your payroll and benefits plans.
- Ask open-ended questions.

- Interview by phone, video conference, or in-person because email exchanges do not provide tone or context of responses to your questions and allow an imposter to find the best answers from someone else's experience disclosed on the internet.
- Establish an hourly or salaried compensation; paying commissions or percentages of grant awards is unethical and, in some places, illegal.
- Verify experience online, inquire about testimonials and references, and ask for proposal samples completed by the grant proposal writer (the grantee's information can be redacted in consideration of confidentiality).
- Partner selectively with a volunteer grant proposal writer because well-intended is not the same as well-experienced. Free isn't always FREE. Although well-intended, an offer to write proposals for free for your organization can end in disaster more times than not. The idea of getting grants written for free might seem like a good idea, but remember, free is often not FREE. While there is no invoice associated with a volunteer effort, a poorly executed attempt can result in not getting much-needed funding, diminished organization reputation, or eliminating the likelihood of being awarded money from that grantmaker in the future because of a less-than-competent submission leaving a lasting unfavorable impression.

It can also result in damaging the relationship the organization has with that volunteer, board member, or staff member. There is also a risk of wasting time and delaying receiving funding because of missing deadlines, unnecessarily long periods of writing and editing proposals, submitting proposals that were not thoroughly researched and vetted, or not being aware of other funding opportunities.

Simply stated, most volunteers, staff, and board members do not know the grant proposal writing process.

- Ensure the grant proposal writer has familiarity with content for the programs/projects and activities in which your organization is engaged.

Some tips for both the nonprofit administrator and contracted grant proposal writer:

- Typical business hours are 9-5, Monday through Friday, unless otherwise stated or established by a working relationship. A working relationship is not established by one handshake or the fact that you have their business card.
- Do not text unless you have established that protocol between the nonprofit administrator and consultant.
- Give the consultant 24 hours to respond to a message. They will receive the message. You do not need to email, call, text, or post on Twitter, Instagram, and LinkedIn within minutes of each other to get their attention.
- No grant proposal writer requires access to website passwords, bank account logins, or accounting systems unless the organization deems it necessary or confers permission. If a grant proposal writer asks for these accesses or permissions, deny it. On occasion, registering to submit or submitting a grant application requires the bank account routing and account numbers. The contract for services can address the process for conveying this information.

As an Executive Director or hiring manager, it is essential to invest in all employees. Supporting and nurturing valuable staff is an investment. Following are a few suggestions to recruit, recognize, and retain a quality grant proposal writer through investment:

- Ensure the salary level reflects the work's demands and the benefits the work brings to the organization and its beneficiaries.
- Grant proposal development obliges involvement from many people within the organization, including board members and key volunteers. Ensure other staff within the organization understand their role in the process and their obligation to participate.
- Ensure the grant proposal writer has up-to-date equipment, appropriate office space, and subscriptions to a high-quality funder database and professional associations.

- Commend victories with an appropriate acknowledgment, and do the same when the proposal does not win the award. Show that you understand the effort made and the emotional let-down of a declined ask.
- Attending quality training and conferences helps staff members stay on top of their game, build professional connections, and reinvigorate their interest in the work. Think of professional development as an essential ingredient in the care and nourishment of an essential organizational resource. Professional development also allows for membership and participation in industry organizations such as the Association of Fundraising Professionals or Grant Professionals Association and obtaining certifications and accreditations in grant proposal writing.

SMART grant proposal writers follow SMART grant proposal criteria:

Specific—The program/project or other funding need is closely tied to the grantmaker's focus and guidelines.

Measurable—Qualitative and quantitative information about inputs, activities, outputs, outcomes, and impacts can be collected.

Achievable—The expected outcomes and impacts support the mission and are realistic.

Relevant—The program/project has an evidence-based design based on a need in the community.

Time-bound—The proposal delineates a period when the funded activities will occur.

Grant proposal writing is about passion, which never acts with an implicit bias regarding any mission. Passion for helping one's own organization or another make a program or project a reality that genuinely proffers change in the community and with all stakeholders. Passion is a little courage, a little crazy, and much diligence. I guess that means that grant proposal writing takes a little courage, a little craziness, and a lot of perseverance. A grant proposal writer does not have to be personally passionate about every mission or program/project for which an application is prepared, but they should be excited and skillful when helping make that mission or program/project successful.

The Program

It is great to read how to refine a craft, such as grant proposal writing. It is even better when there are examples and samples from which to train and learn. The standard practice in training is to provide authentic illustrations and archetypes. The standard is also that a variety of examples are presented, but this standard creates little or no continuity for training or lessons covering multiple chapters or blocks. There is no frame of reference from which to build. Variety can be good, but continuity provides for better understanding as well as a foundation from which to build.

Throughout *SMART Money Grant Writing*, one program—the same program—is used for every example and sample. The choice of program is comprehensive, scalable, user-friendly, relevant, and practical. With any program, each of us could find ways that we might do things differently (and that is precisely how we should be thinking). This is a fictitious organization and program. However, all the information is adapted from existing nonprofit programs, operations, staffing, volunteers, and other resources to make serving a community possible.

Organization: Mentoring Individuals with Disabilities (MIWD)

Mentoring Individuals with Disabilities is a 501(c)3, and the EIN is 81-55533321. The physical and mailing addresses are the same, 1234 Main St., Johnsontown, Ohio 45000. MIWD was established in and has been providing programs and services since 2013. MIWD offers job development activities for people with disabilities who seek employment.

Mission Statement: Helping individuals with disabilities secure integrated, sustainable, living-wage employment for increased independence and enhanced lifestyle.

Program: Flip It Reverse Job and Career Fair
Flip It Reverse Job and Career Fair is for individuals with disabilities who want to be working and companies with a need for talented, qualified employees.

The vision of the program is to connect job seekers with disabilities with business owners and hiring managers by turning the tables on the traditional job fair. These connections will create job and career opportunities with sustainable, living wages for employees with disabilities while filling critical roles within companies with qualified individuals from an underutilized talent pool.

Principles of Progress:
- Empower job seekers with disabilities with increased self-reliance and economic independence
- Gain integrity through the efficient and responsible use of all funds and personnel for the Flip It program
- Invite the opportunity to share in collaborative partnerships
- Deliver measurable and comprehensive project(s) with results to all stakeholders
- Advance our communities through decreased reliance on assistance programs, positive economic impacts through increased tax base via income taxes and local spending
- Challenge ourselves to realize our promise and potential for disability inclusion across all business and economic sectors of our community

Flip It - Concept:
The purpose is that every job seeker with disabilities will have an opportunity to showcase their skills, personality, and ambition to prospective employers in an

environment that is more comfortable and accommodating than in traditional interview settings for a rewarding and successful interview process for the job seekers and employers alike. Job development assistance with resumes, mock interviews, display boards, job development-related soft skills, and interview process milestones is offered to benefit the job seeker as well as provide support to job developers and job development programs in the community. Creating awareness about the return on investment of employees with disabilities throughout the business community will dispel myths about disability inclusion and improve businesses' bottom lines by decreased turnover, more robust attendance rates, greater productivity, and improved overall company morale.

How will we accomplish this?

1. By providing access to and facilitating comprehensive job development activities to benefit job seekers with disabilities and their support teams (family, friends, vocational rehabilitation professionals, job developers, and job coaches) as well as business owners and hiring managers through workshops and forums
2. By providing increased (business) community awareness through facts about disability inclusion in the workplace to dispel myths about costs, company culture, and attendance and turnover rates of employees with disabilities
3. By providing Central Ohio businesses with partnership opportunities, including education and training about disability inclusion with bi-monthly panels, event participants and sponsors, in-kind donations, and Volunteer Time Off (VTO) program
4. By providing valuable assistance to job development programs and professionals (and other job seeker support team members) in Central Ohio through Resume Reboot, Tell Me About It (mock interviews and 30-second elevator speech rehearsals), Dress for Success, Display Board Build, and Job and Career Seeking Process Must-Dos for their consumers
5. April 20XX reverse job & career fair

6. Disability etiquette infographics, videos
7. Volunteer training, including etiquette video

Flip It will turn the tables on hiring events in Central Ohio in October 20XX. The October event is timely to bring additional attention to National Disability Employment Awareness Month. Job Seeker Registration begins July 1, 20XX, with business owners and hiring managers registration starting July 15th.

Please contact us now to partner as a sponsor and with other support at 614-555-8246, email tnystrom@miwd.org, and visit www.miwd.org.

Program Components –
1. Job and Career Fair—20-30 8' or 40 6' clothed tables, bottled water, healthy snacks, meeting room space, convenient to bus line, 11 am-3 pm
2. Speaker Corner—Motivational Speakers and Subject Matter Experts with Disabilities can promote their platform and programs(s)
3. Resume Reboot—1 week before job and career fair, 4 hours, library meeting room, templates on the website
4. Tell Me About It (mock Interviews and 30-second elevator speech rehearsals)—1 week before job and career fair, 4 hours, library meeting room, sample questions template
5. Dress for Success (interview and career wardrobe assistance)—2 weeks before job and career fair
6. Display Board Build (presentation boards available to create at no charge)—1 week before job and career fair, 4 hours, library meeting room, supplies provided
7. Employer Forum—one community event 2 weeks before job and career fair, and one day from 10-10:45 am; available upon request for groups, organizations, leadership teams
8. VR/JD Professionals Information Packet and Video
9. Volunteer orientation—via email, webcast/YouTube Video

10. Disability Inclusion Training Handbook—all participants, business/hiring attendees, sponsors, volunteers
11. Transportation stipend—2 one-day bus passes per participant, $4.00 parking for Main Library venue, up to $10 day of reimbursement via reimbursement form
12. Sponsor Packages—two tiers, employee volunteer hours options (limited to need, first come/first served for companies)
13. Media and marketing plan
14. Vocational focus color/symbol coding to assist employers

Executive Summary

MENTORING INDIVIDUALS WITH DISABILITIES PROPOSES TO INCREASE THE RETURN OF INVESTMENT ON DISABILITY INCLUSION

Mentoring Individuals with Disabilities(MIWD), 501(c)3, is looking to increase the already fervent support from disability agencies and the business community in order to provide this innovative mentoring experience by creating greater familiarity with the Return on Investment (ROI of disability diversity in the workplace. The experience helps job seekers with disabilities develop the necessary skills and experiences they'll need to compete in today's competitive workforce while assisting area companies in securing some of the most dedicated employees in the Columbus, Ohio market.

While the unemployment rate for people with disabilities recently was reported at its lowest in three years, the Allsup Disability Study: Income at Risk reports that people with disabilities experienced an unemployment rate nearly 65% higher than the rate for people with no disabilities for the second quarter of 2018. As a result of MIWD, this employment inequity will be reduced as individuals with disabilities will:

- Increase earnings and earning potential
- Increase the likelihood of securing health care benefits
- Increase self-esteem. self-worth, and independence
- Increase inclusion through social and professional opportunities
- Reduce dependency on public and private vocational rehabilitation programs

Mentoring Individuals with Disabilities assists individuals with disabilities with person-centered job development activities for sustained, competitive employment. The program connects employees of varied physical and mental disabilities with employers through career exploration experiences at local businesses interested in diversifying their human resources recruitment on an ongoing basis. Mentoring Individuals with Disabilities Day underscores the impacts of the ongoing program pursuits. MIWD Day is a community-awareness building event held quarterly, focusing on sustainable, competitive employment for individuals with disabilities. MIWD seeks to match mentees/job seekers) with area businesses offering job shadowing and hands-on career exploration. Additional informational events are provided in October, National Disability Employment Awareness Month.

Employers have the opportunity to conduct the Americans with Disabilities Act (ADA) and disability etiquette training for management and employees in their workplace as part of this program because familiarity and knowledge eliminate barriers. Employers are provided with extensive ROI of Disability information and marketing support to display in the workplace. Mentees are matched on a first-come, first-served basis in areas of their vocational goals and interests. A reception celebrating the event will be hosted at the end of the workday, honoring our mentees, mentors, business partners, sponsors, and volunteers.

The combination of the Mentoring Individuals with Disabilities programs and Mentoring Individuals with Disabilities Day allows MIWD to apportion awareness that despite the additional obstacles that people with disabilities confront, they want to work and earn a sustaining, living-wage income.

SWOT Analysis—MIWD
Flip It Reverse Job and Career Fair

STRENGTHS	WEAKNESSES
• No competition • Disability inclusion is a broader initiative than ever before • Comprehensive program components • Developed with vocational rehabilitation professionals • Job seekers with disabilities participating in VR job development programs or not can participate • Robust volunteer engagement in the community • Business community indicates the need and desire for DI information and engagement	• Nonprofit is a young organization • Lack of familiarity with reverse job and career fair model • Trends in VR job development models • Competitive environment for cause-driven funding and sponsorships • Myths about hiring people with disabilities
OPPORTUNITIES	THREATS
• No competition • Traditional full- and part-time job opportunities • Increased awareness of the return on investment of employees with disabilities • Securing community and funding partners	• Flip It Reverse Job and Career Fair is a new opportunity in the area • Economy • Competitive environment for cause-driven funding and sponsorships • Lack of familiarity with reverse job and career fair model

Budget: Flip It Reverse Job and Career Fair	
Expenses	$$$
Job fair venue	800
Venues—Resume Reboot, Tell Me About It, Dress for Success, Display Board Build, Employer Forum, Wrap-up	0
Supplies and equipment	1,260
Transporation stipends, mileage reimbursement	400
Website	94
Bottled water, healthy snacks—all events	65
Salaries—program manager	12,295
Fringe benefits	0
Disability inclusion handbooks	1,184
Utilities, office space	0
In-kind goods and services	1,735
TOTAL	17,833
Funding Strategy (Revenue)	$$$
Grants	8,500
Weisenberger Family Foundation	5,000
Rolston Pipe and Tool Grant Program	3,500
Association for Disability Employment	2,000 (pending)
Human Resources Professionals of Ohio	1,000 (pending)
Sponsorships	3,923
In-kind donations	1,735
Private donations	3,674
TOTAL	17,833
Volunteer Value = # x $27.20*	1,360 value

About the Author—Tarra Nystrom, MBA, CBA

I am a writer, author, freelancer, Mom, advocate for disability inclusion, seamstress, business owner, communication strategist, and humorist. I have more than 35 years of writing, communication, and marketing experience as a small business owner and consultant to other entrepreneurs. I began my professional career in the hotel industry, specifically catering and event planning. From there, I built an award-winning special events company for more than 20 years in Baltimore, MD, and Columbus, OH, and later found additional success in nonprofit management and grant proposal writing.

Public speaking, industry instructor, writing tutor, published author, and (Baltimore's) Best Party Decor are some of my career accomplishments. I am the Mother of two compassionate, accomplished, and witty adult children. I am an enthusiastic alumnus of The Ohio State University, earning a BA in Strategic Communication; and an MBA from Ohio Dominican University. Proudly, I am also a Certified Balloon Artist.

I know that successful grant applications seamlessly integrate compelling stories with facts and statistics. My grant proposal writing presents thorough research and humanizes the material making client proposals stand out from the competition. My collaborative and transparent approach evolved by understanding that every organization has specific funding goals and is at various staffing and expertise stages. I've been working in nonprofits and writing grant proposals for 12 years, helping nonprofits, for-profits, and individuals secure more than $11 million in grants. I have trained more than 360 nonprofit professionals in grant proposal writing and related topics. For more information, please visit SMARTMoneyGrantWriting.com.

Tarra's titles:

SMART Money Grant Writing: Case Statements for Nonprofits (2023)

SMART Money Grant Writing: Ready-to-Use Writing (2022)

SMART Money Grant Writing Workbook (2022)

Nonfiction for Nonprofit: Use Your Nonprofit's Story to Elevate the Organization and Generate Revenue (2021)

SMART Money Grant Writing: Get the Funding Your Organization Needs and Deserves (2020)

The DisABILITY A-Player Plan: Employee of the Month Every Month (2016)

DIY: Balloon Sculptures: Really Cool Balloon Sculptures for the Holidays! (2014)

DIY Balloon Sculptures: Really Cool Balloon Sculptures You Can Make Yourself! (2013)

SMART Money Grant Writing:

Get the Funding Your Organization Needs and Deserves

www.ingramcontent.com/pod-product-compliance
Lightning Source LLC
Chambersburg PA
CBHW080411170426
43194CB00015B/2782